AN ARCHAEOLOGICAL INVENTORY OF BRANTLEY RESERVOIR, NEW MEXICO

MODELS OF REGIONAL CULTURE HISTORY

by

Mark   Henderson

Southern Methodist University
Institute for the Study of Earth and Man
Department of Anthropology

Report submitted to the National Park Service by the Archaeology Research Program, Southern Methodist University in fulfillment of Contract No. CX700040177.

1976: DEPARTMENT OF ANTHROPOLOGY, SOUTHERN METHODIST UNIVERSITY

Distributed by the Archaeology Research Program, Department of Anthropology,

Southern Methodist University, Dallas, Texas 75275 U.S.A.

SOUTHERN METHODIST UNIVERSITY CONTRIBUTIONS IN ANTHROPOLOGY, No. 18

ABSTRACT

An archaeological survey in a relatively un-studied section of southeastern New Mexico has located 92 archaeological sites, 77 of which were prehistoric and 15 of which were occupied within the last century. Four separate models are discussed centering on different levels of investigation. One model attempts a synthesis of environmental change and cultural responses in the Middle Pecos region. A second model investigates an ethnographic example of aboriginal occupation in the Middle Pecos and proposes ways in which this knowledge may be made into a predictive model for prehistoric subsistence and settlement systems. A third model investigates a site typology and functional explanation for prehistoric sites in the Brantley Reservoir survey sample of sites. A fourth model investigates the patterned variability of artifacts on one specific site in the survey area which was partially collected in controlled grid units. These four models correspond fairly closely with differing levels of abstraction and proposed directions for further study in the mitigation of destruction of archaeological resources to be affected by Brantley Reservoir.

ACKNOWLEDGEMENTS

It is odd that the acknowledgements to a piece of (hopefully) scientific research should turn out to be so difficult to write. It is surely a sign of poor research that does not owe a debt of some kind to a great many people. On the other hand, anyone who reflects on the issue and is pleased to acknowledge the help and contribution of everyone who has had some part in the research enterprise quickly finds how frustrating it is to thank everyone adequately. I would like to think that a true accounting of indebtedness leading to the fruition of this volume would run into several volumes of a similar weight. It would include several levels of inclusivity, probably starting with my utmost debt to the great Mountains and open spaces of the Western United States which, until recently, humanity (to which I am also indebted) has seen fit to preserve in an unmatched state of beauty and natural wonder. Somewhere in this category I would have to include my parents and family who provided both the physical and intellectual tools with which to better appreciate the phenomena of man and nature. And so I would go on acknowledging and thanking until anyone who was an addicted reader of acknowledgements would lose interest before they even began to peruse the pages of "research" which are presented here. For this reason I have settled on a somewhat attenuated form of acknowledgement. I hope that all of those whom I have overlooked can appreciate the sacrifice of completeness for the sake of brevity.

First of all I would like to thank William B. Fawcett, Jr. as a friend and able assistant in the field. In the same vein I would like to thank the crew of the Brantley Survey: Debbie Thompson, Gabriella Uhlar, John Landon, Edwin Kiser, David Rutledge, and Dick Detwiler. Together I think we achieved tolerable success in completing an inventory survey of the archaeological resources of Brantley Reservoir.

Several long-time residents of the southeastern New Mexico area were of immeasurable help because of their knowledge and willingness to share information about the history and prehistory of their home range. Mr. William (Bill) Balgeman of the Zoological Botanical State Park of the Southwest deserves a great deal of indebtedness for promoting the cause of natural history in this corner of New Mexico and also personal indebtedness for his unflagging enthusiasm and donation of time in helping us to better cover the ground. Similarly, Mr. Lee Myers of Carlsbad and Mrs. Frances White Collins of the Artesia Historical Museum have continued to be invaluable in their personal efforts to preserve historic materials and in their willingness to share these with others.

Mr. and Mrs. John Runyan and Mr. Robert Leslie of the Lea County Archeological Society all have contributed thoughtfully in the field and laboratory and with encouragement and hospitality in times of need.

Mr. Francis Tracy of the Carlsbad Irrigation District and Mr. Baer of the Artesia Chamber of Commerce provided a refuge and repository of important information at many crucial points during our stay.

To Mr. Forrest Lee goes a great deal of admiration on the part of the whole crew. I hope his disappointment in not finding Patty Hearst among us is recompensed in part by the friendship of the crew and the completion of this report.

Several people in the Archaeology Research Program and Anthropology Department at SMU have also been essential in the laboratory research phase of this report. Dr. S. Alan Skinner, Principal Investigator for this project and Director of the Archaeology Research Program, has been instrumental in creating an atmosphere for improving the quality of salvage, contract, and conservation archaeology. The production of this report in many ways reflects his ideas and thinking about archaeological research. Mr. Joseph G. Gallagher of the Archaeology Research Program provided many additional stimulating ideas and particularly suggested the stem width measure as a possible chronometric device, at least for heuristic purposes. Mr. Richard Larson of the Archaeology Research Program was able to impart some of his statistical expertise to the author. This little bit of knowledge is dangerous; any errors and misuses of statistical techniques are entirely my own.

Mr. Dale Edleman of the Geology Department, the University of Texas at Dallas, performed the pollen analysis and to him also go my thanks.

I would also like to thank the pre-publication reviewers of this report: Dr. Susan M. Applegarth, Chairman, Department of Anthropology, Fort Lewis College; Mr. Paul R. Katz and Ms. Susanna R. Katz, University of Texas, San Antonio; Dr. Jane Kelley, Department of Archaeology, University of Calgary; Ms. Anne Loose, Staff Archeologist, Roswell District, Bureau of Land Management; Mr. Lee Myers, Carlsbad; Mr. and Mrs. John W. Runyan, Lea County Archeological Society, Hobbs; and Mr. Regge N. Wiseman, Staff Archeologist, Laboratory of Anthropology. I am sorry that I have been unable to include more of the changes that were suggested to improve the accuracy and completeness of this report. All the errors of fact or interpretation are, of course, due to my own shortcomings.

Several technical tasks have seemed endless to me but must have seemed even more so to others. For forging ahead in spite of the syntactic, grammatical, and semantic difficulties in my rendition of English, I would like to thank: Meg Rohrt for typing and editing, Natalie Kern for editing and graphics, and Anne Justen for the final editing. Leta Smith and Charlotte Archer deserve credit for drafting maps and charts and Hubie Achor for the photographic layouts. The typesetting, done on IBM equipment, and page paste-up were done by personnel in the Graphics Lab, Department of Anthropology, Institute for the Study of Earth and Man, Southern Methodist University.

Finally, Yolanda Vigil-Henderson, my wife, deserves recognition for the structure of all phases of this research. Besides being a regular member of the survey team she was also a fine chef for nine people as well as an unusually insightful advisor. Without her help archaeology would lose its meaning and this report would be much less complete.

CONTENTS

CONTENTS (Cont.)

FIGURES

TABLES

INTRODUCTION

This monograph reports the findings of an archaeological site inventory survey of the proposed Brantley Reservoir, to be located on the Pecos River between the towns of Carlsbad and Artesia in southeastern New Mexico. The area covered by the archaeological survey reported here is on an ecotone between a finger of the Chihuahuan Desert, a sparse grassland environment associated with the Llano Estacado immediately to the east, and basin and range topography on the perimeter of the Colorado Plateau to the north and west.

The archaeology of the conjunction of these three environmental zones is poorly understood, and the recognition of these zones provides a sound basis from which to begin work on the past cultural conditions in the survey area. Although an absolute homology between environmental region and cultural group is unlikely, the relationship between behavior and environment can be used as a central concept for investigating the archaeology of southeastern New Mexico. Formulating such a concept will show that empirical studies of both ecology and the material remains of past human activity in this area at present can neither confirm nor reject the suggested relationship between environment and culture.

A number of recent studies have summarized the archaeology of parts of southeastern New Mexico (Burns 1967; Riches 1970; Kelley 1966; Marshall 1973). Because of the lack of quantitative information and the largely descriptive nature of these reports, it is unnecessary to review in detail all the archaeological work that has been undertaken in the Middle Pecos River Basin region.

Outlined here are the major developments in the region as they relate to the interaction of the three broad geographical/environmental regions mentioned above. This discussion will start with a more detailed consideration of environment as it exists today in the Middle Pecos, and subsequently a preliminary effort will be made to reconstruct the climate and climatic changes through time. Later on, an in-depth discussion will occur on the specifics of the archaeological survey of the Brantley Reservoir.

The research which this report represents was undertaken as partial fulfillment of the National Environmental Policy Act of 1969 which requires multidisciplinary study of the environmental impact of Federal construction projects. The study area, referred to as the Seven Rivers area, included land to be directly and indirectly affected by the construction of the proposed Brantley Dam and Reservoir (fig. 1), designed by the Bureau of Reclamation for flood control, irrigation, and recreational purposes. The area in which the dam is to be located obviously was not chosen as a unit of study for its representativeness of archaeological materials on the Middle Pecos River. However, the area (approximately 30,000 acres in extent) does have a significant archaeological occupation which upon further investigation will provide an important addition to the understanding of southeastern New Mexico archaeology.

The area presents a challenge beyond the adequate mitigation of loss of archaeological remains that will be destroyed by reservoir construction. This challenge is to reconstruct the nature of human occupation in an area where several cultural traditions at different times interfinger at the conjunction of three rather distinct biotic areas. This relationship should be more fully understood at the conclusion of archaeological research in the Seven Rivers area. The archaeological record within the Seven Rivers area is complex, and there is

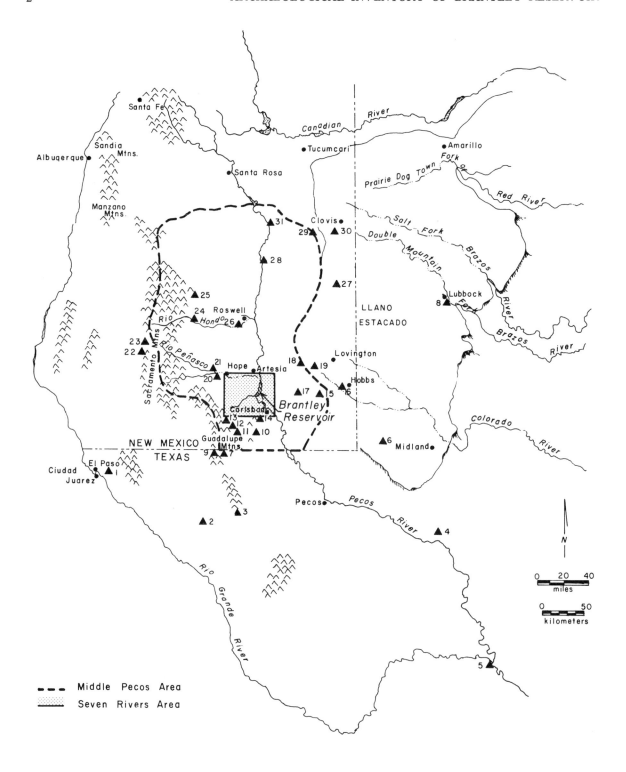

FIG. 1—Selected Archaeological Sites and Geographic Localities in Southeastern New Mexico and Western Texas.

evidence for human usage of the area for the last 10,000 years. Portions of this record are to be found at 92 archaeological sites in the reservoir area. In a fashion which seems to be characteristic of the Middle Pecos Valley bottom, no single site within the survey area seems to be neatly layered like a geological column.

Adequate mitigation of the loss of archaeological resources, an understanding of climatic processes as they affect culture, and determining processes of culture change are all objectives of the study of the archaeology in Brantley Reservoir. This survey report is simply a first step in fulfilling these goals. Future detailed excavation should fill out our understanding of the human ecology of the Seven Rivers area over the last 10,000 years and contribute something to our relatively limited understanding of the culture history of southeastern New Mexico.

LEGEND FOR FIG. 1
Localities and Sites Discussed in Text

1—*Pow Wow Site*—Greer (1968a, 1968b)
2—*MILE HIGH*—Skinner, Steed, and Bearden (1973)
3—*Three Mile-Sulphur*—Skinner and Bousman (1973)
4—*Parker Ranch*—Sommer (1968)
5—*Bonfire Shelter*—Bryant (1969), Dibble (1968)
6—*Andrews Lake: Salt Cedar Site*—Collins (1968)
7—*Guadalupe Mountains*—Katz and Katz (1974), Shafer (1970)
8—*Lubbock Lake Site*—Black (1974)
9—*Williams Cave*—Ayer (1936)
10—*Carlsbad Caverns National Park*—Greer (1966), Bousman (1974a), Bradley (1959)
11—*Hermit's Cave*—Ferdon (1946), Haynes (1967)
12—*Burnet Cave*—Howard (1935)
13—*Mera's Reconnaissance*—Mera (1938)
14—*Honest Injun Cave*—Riches (1970), Applegarth (1975)
15—*Merchant Site*—Leslie (1965)
16—*Monument Spring Site*—Leslie (1968)

17—*Laguna Plata Site*—Runyan (1972)
18—*Boot Hill Site*—Corley and Leslie (1960)
19—*Rattlesnake Draw*—Smith, East-Smith, and Runyan (1966)
20—*Wolf Creek Canyon Ranch*—Hafsten (1961)
21—*LA 2000-2002*—Jennings (1940)
22—*Fresnal Shelter*—Human Systems Research (1973, 1974)
23—*Bent Project*—Wiseman (1973)
24—*Glencoe Project*—Broilo (1973)
25—*Sierra Blanca Region*—Kelley (1966)
26—*Bloom Mound*—Ross (1969), Kelley (1966)
27—*Milnesand*—Sellards (1955), Warnica and Williamson (1968)
28—*Middle Pecos Survey*—Jelinek (1967)
29—*Billy the Kid Cave*—Kunz, Gamache, and Agogino (1973), Kunz (1969)
30—*Blackwater Draw*—Wendorf and Hester (1975)
31—*Ft. Sumner*—Wilson (1967)
32—*Mayhill*—Green (1956)

NATURAL ENVIRONMENT OF THE MIDDLE PECOS BASIN

POSITION AND BOUNDARY
OF ECOLOGICAL PROVINCE

The Middle Pecos has been defined as the region drained by the Pecos River and its tributaries between Alamogordo Reservoir (now Fort Sumner Reservoir) on the north and the New Mexico–Texas state line on the south (U. S. National Resources Planning Board 1942: 135). This region is situated at an ecotone between several biogeographic provinces. While quantitative demonstration of the existence of an ecotone within the area to be covered by the Brantley Reservoir is lacking, several qualitative observations and an analysis of the effects of geology on the distribution of animals and particularly plants indicate the existence of an ecotone in the area (Jaeger 1957: 35; Blair 1950).

INTERRELATIONSHIP
OF NATURAL SYSTEMS

Whether or not environmental conditions are active or passive shapers of culture, a thorough knowledge of these conditions is of importance in trying to reconstruct past cultural systems. In a similar sense, the geological and abiotic structure of a region are of crucial importance to understanding the animal and plant populations established there. The plant and animal populations are systematically related to the geology of the area. In turn, the structure and nature of living communities affect the soils and geology.

GEOLOGY AND TOPOGRAPHY
OF THE MIDDLE PECOS

Major Geologic Processes

Several important professional geological studies have been carried out in the Middle Pecos Basin, and some of these studies are crucial to an understanding of the present and past economies of the basin. The studies are largely concerned with deep rock phenomena relating to the rich petroleum industry of the Llano Estacado and the Permian Basin (Hayes 1964). Other studies have focused more specifically on hydrological resources of the Roswell Artesian Basin (Fiedler and Nye 1933). These studies have a bearing on the understanding of the prehistoric human economy by providing evidence of change in hydrologic patterns in the Middle Pecos. Speleological phenomena of the Capitan Reef have also generated a considerable interest in the regional tectonics of the Middle Pecos (Horberg 1949).

In terms of rapid modification of ecological conditions, the geologic processes operating on the Middle Pecos Basin have been relatively undramatic. The major shapers of the current topograpy have been a general regional uplift of the Capitan Reef from Permian seas and the formation of associated erosional surfaces, solution caverns, and stream courses resulting from hydrologic patterns in the Middle Pecos and nearby regions. Vulcanism or igneous processes are evidenced in the hard rock geology of the Middle Pecos drainage only in the Sierra Blanca volcanics (Kelley 1971: 29). The significance of drainage patterns and their shifts emerge as the most critical topographic variable affecting changes in human populations.

Overall Topographic Structure

Large topographic features have structured geologic processes in the Seven Rivers area, but clearly the reverse is also true. The Seven Rivers join and flow into the Pecos just north of a series of hills and an escarpment called the Seven Rivers Hills (Cuesta). The hills trend northeast-southwest and form the northeasternmost exposure of the Capitan Reef formations (Hayes 1964: 4). The Seven Rivers Hills also mark the southern edge of the Roswell Artesian Basin (Fiedler and Nye 1933: 17). At the point where the Seven Rivers Hills abut the Pecos, another "southeastward-plunging syncline" is recognized (Meinzer, Renick, and Bryan 1927: 15). These converging synclines mark the border between a more northerly basin dominated by a drainage pattern associated with the Sacramento Mountains and a southerly basin dominated by the Guadalupe Mountains. The artesian systems of these two basins are apparently distinct (Fiedler and Nye 1933: 156). Geologic developments in these two basins may eventually be tied to the timing of the solution-subsidence and piracy of the Pecos in the Pleistocene. At the convergence of these basins, the proposed Brantley Dam will be constructed.

The possibly independent subsidence of the basins may be related to changes in surface water supplies of the area. Fiedler and Nye (1933: 102) suggest that a recent change in the Peñasco drainage has moved the course of the river from entering the Pecos north of Artesia to south of Artesia. The cause of this movement may be a gradual southeastward plunge of the Roswell Artesian Basin. The timing of this change may be significant to the human use of the Peñasco River in the Brantley Reservoir area. Again, the archaeology of the area may indicate when this change occurred. No archaeological materials could be associated with the current Peñasco drainage within the Seven Rivers survey area. This may be significant in light of recent changes in the topography of the Roswell Basin.

Stream Capture and Piracy

At the beginning of the Pleistocene, southeastern New Mexico looked topographically much as it does today. The Sacramento and Guadalupe Mountain massifs were present. The eastward-sloping pediments of these ranges were similarly dissected by many eastward-flowing streams and arroyos. This dissected surface on the east flank of the Sacramento Mountains is known as the Diamond A Plain (Feidler and Nye 1933: 14). During the early Pleistocene, the Diamond A Plain continued to the east beyond the current Texas–New Mexico border unbroken by the north/south–flowing Pecos drainage. Gradually, headward erosion began to occur on the Pecos by solution subsidence. The Pecos worked its way north, pirating stream after stream flowing out of the western ranges. The Seven Rivers may have been part of the Pecos drainage before extensive headward erosion began; but subsequently, the Peñasco, Hondo, and the ancient Portales River that flowed through Blackwater Draw were captured. Evidence indicates that the Portales River was captured by the Pecos sometime in the Late Pleistocene (Reeves 1972: 113). It is uncertain when this process affected the Seven Rivers and the Peñasco drainages. This rate of change problem, which warranted attention over 25 years ago, is still unsolved (Horberg 1949; Bretz and Horberg 1949; Reeves 1972).

The Stream Terrace System

Study of the Pleistocene river terrace development may elucidate the sequence and timing of the pirating process. Fiedler and Nye (1933: 10-13) hypothesize the existence of three terraces along the Pecos within the Roswell Artesian Basin. These terraces are (from most recent to oldest)—the Lakewood, the Blackdom, and the Orchard Park. The type locality of the Lakewood Terrace is to be covered by Brantley Lake. The Blackdom Terrace is recognizable as the rising land which will form the shores of the reservoir. To the north the development of these terraces is more complex, and their chronological placement needs further examination (Reeves 1972: 11).

A case can be made for dating these terraces on the basis of archaeological remains. The timing of terrace development along the entire Pecos River may be elucidated by locations of archaeological remains (Jelinek 1967: 9-10). For example, Jelinek (1967: 16-17) notes that:

> Permanent or semipermanent settlements were restricted to the well-drained Blackdom and Orchard Park terrace surfaces and are most frequently encountered where these surfaces are within a few hundred feet of the river.

In the Seven Rivers area the survey recovered no evidence of "permanent settlements." However, sites with Paleo-Indian or early Archaic materials were consistently located on the upper two terraces (Blackdom or Orchard Park), but sites on the most highly developed section of the lower terrace (Lakewood) yielded no Paleo-Indian or Archaic materials. In almost every instance some pottery was present on the Lakewood Terrace sites. This may indicate that the lower terrace (the Lakewood) was not available for settlement in Archaic and Paleo-Indian times. Fiedler and Nye (1933: 11) state that the Lakewood Terrace never floods. However, farmers report it has flooded several times since 1940 and mention finding sediments burying tops of fence posts. This flooding apparently is still aggrading portions of Lakewood Terrace. Further study of the correlation of terrace deposits with cultural developments may help in interpreting large-scale developments in Quaternary geology on the Pecos River.

Eolian Processes

Alluvial processes and the structures that affect them are not the sole geological shapers of the region. Eolian materials occur in the Seven Rivers area as well. Sand dunes are particularly visible on the flanks of the Pecos River below McMillan Dam. Dune activity also occurs in the more open areas east of the Pecos. These dunes appear to be shifting today while the dunes along the river are stabilized by dense mesquite growth.

The actual geologic and associational history of these dunes is uncertain (Reeves 1972: 111-12). The fact that they appear to be derived from a reddish sandstone would tie them to formations on the Mescalero Ridge or other sandstone formations rather than to limestone formations. This eolian activity is more typical of the Llano Estacado to the east than to activity in the Roswell Artesian Basin. Reeves (1972: 111-12) suggests that the sand dunes can be tied to the larger regional dune formation events which created the Monahans or Judkins deposits near Midland, Texas as well as elsewhere on the Llano Estacado.

Summary of Geologic Conditions

In this broad context the geology of the Seven Rivers area can be characterized by describing the major topographic features. The Pecos River forms the heart of the present area flanked by a series of broadly spaced terraces. The two upper terraces (Orchard Park and Blackdom) are largely outside the area to be affected by dam construction; however, they contain the only native stone in the area. On top of the latter can be found some reworked Ogallala gravels (Bretz and Horberg 1949) that were used for chipped stone implements. The Seven Rivers Hills paired with the McMillan Escarpment (Hayes 1964: 4) on the southern limit of the area (see fig. 2) form a rather narrow neck through which the Pecos flows out of the Roswell Artesian Basin. The Permian dolomite, of which the major topographic features are composed, is the only abundant lithic resource in the area. The rapid

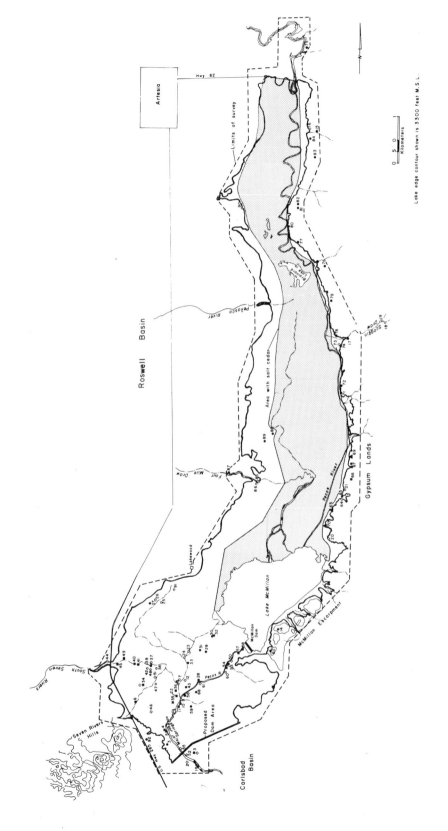

FIG. 2.—Location of Archaeological Sites* and Major Topographic Features About Brantley Reservoir. ■—Artifact and Burned Rock Scatter (Large) Sites; ○—Artifact and Burned Rock Scatter (Small) Sites; ▲—Artifact Scatter (Large) Sites; ●—Artifact Scatter (Small) Sites; ◇—Historic Sites. (*All site numbers are preceded by X29ED).

water solution of dolomite has resulted in a rounded profile in the Seven Rivers Hills area. These water-soluble materials are prone to the formation of solution cavities when surface water stands or flows nearby. Eolian and alluvial filling apparently prevented the use of these cavities as shelter over long periods in the immediate area of Brantley Reservoir. Eolian materials are deposited on the floodplain. This activity also occurs on the thin soils of the gypsum and dolomite bedrock of the uplands. The bedrock outcrops, the sand dunes, and the river terraces set the stage for the plant and animal associations in the reservoir area.

GEOLOGY AND TOPOGRAPHY OF THE SEVEN RIVERS AREA

Major Topographic Features

The Seven Rivers Hills and the McMillan Escarpment (Hayes 1964) form the northeastern finger of the Capitan Reef structure in its surface manifestation (see fig. 2). The Pecos River dissects the last joint of this finger, and across this gap Brantley Dam will be constructed. The McMillan Escarpment warps down as it begins to parallel the Pecos River running north from the gap. This dolomitic Capitan Reef finger disappears as it follows the river north. Caliche and sand deposits form the more gently rising terrain east of the river. The escarpment on the east side of the Pecos from the gap to almost due east of Artesia is steeply faced, abruptly rising terrain. It gradually turns into a gently rising to the caprock of the Llano Estacado to the east.

The south and east sides of the Seven Rivers Hills area are demarcated rather distinctly by the features discussed above. From the north and west, the Seven Rivers flow from the Diamond A Plain onto the bottomlands in the Brantley Reservoir region. Close to the Pecos River, the Seven Rivers flow in an incised channel. In the bottomlands flanking this channel is the type location of the Lakewood Terrace (Fiedler and Nye 1933: 10). This terrace forms about 90 to 95% of the area that will be flooded by Brantley Reservoir. The terrace extends mostly on the west side of the Pecos River forming a plain across which the channels of the Seven Rivers have been incised.

Soils and Vegetation

Landforms as described for the area by Fiedler and Nye (1933) correspond closely with the soil associations mapped for this vicinity by the Soil Conservation Service (U. S. Department of Agriculture 1971).

The Reeves-Gypsum Association, which coincides with the gypsum beds to the north, is dominated by creosote bush but may also contain a series of specially adapted flora in undisturbed sections (Waterfall 1946). The Ector Association occurring on the Seven Rivers Hills and McMillan Escarpment on the southern and eastern border of the reservoir is also dominated primarily by creosote but may be slightly more variable in secondary floristic dominants. The Arno–Harkey–Anthony Association, corresponding to the Lakewood Terrace in the center of the reservoir area, seems to have two components: a loose sandy soil dominated by mesquite, with some datil, cactus, and other shrubs; and a silty, seasonally moist component dominated by tamarisk (salt cedar) or cultivated plants. Also bordering the deep soils of the Lakewood Terrace on the west and marginally within the area is the Reagon-Upton Soil Association with deep soils and stony slopes and a vegetation regime very similar to the sandy fraction of the Arno–Harkey–Anthony soils. This area corresponds topographically to the Orchard Park Terrace of Fiedler and Nye (1933).

This picture of the soils and vegetation in the Seven Rivers area is generalized. The botany of the area was not studied during the survey, and a systematic inventory of plants should be undertaken in the area to help understand soil and vegetation variability. The fact that much of the modern vegetation may be a result of environmental changes over the last 100 years should also be held carefully in mind. The dominant vegetation in all these areas (mesquite, creosote, and tamarisk) is demonstrated to be due to recent changes in most of west Texas and southern New Mexico (Gardner 1950; Campbell 1929; Harris 1966). This vegetation replaces dominant climax grassland vegetation (Gardner 1950; Harris 1966).

Hydrology

Water resources also seem to have been more abundant before 1870 when the first white settlers entered the area. Currently there are several springs in the reservoir area. One emerges from under the gypsum soils on the east side of the Pecos in Chalk Bluff Draw and was producing small amounts of water even after a dry season. The other is a series of springs which emerge directly into the Pecos. This series of springs, called Major Johnson Springs, is directly linked to the water seeping out of Lake McMillan and emerging about ten days later and two miles (7 km) downstream (U. S. National Resources Planning Board 1942).

Lake McMillan itself retains variable amounts of water within the area. The Pecos River becomes dry when water is not being released from Lake McMillan until seepage water from the lake emerges downstream at Major Johnson Springs. Evidence for formerly greater amounts of ground water in the area is good. Fiedler and Nye (1933) document the rather dramatic lowering of ground water supplies throughout the Roswell Artesian Basin. The Artesian head has been lowered systematically so that today all water in the region must be pumped even in the lowest parts of the basin. Indications of former springs were found in several places during the survey

where homesteads built in the 1870s or 1880s had been abandoned. In addition, descendants of pioneer families have indicated that the Seven Rivers, Fourmile Draw, and the Peñasco River formerly were permanently flowing streams. Today only the extreme lower course of the Seven Rivers is consistently wet, and this may be due to irrigation seepage or overflows. Indications are that not only has the grassland been modified, but also the riparian environment that bordered these watercourses has changed.

VEGETATION OF THE MIDDLE PECOS RIVER BASIN

Vegetative Provinces

The intersection of three generally recognized biotic provinces occurs in the Seven Rivers vicinity. These are the Kansan, Navahonian, and Chihuahuan biotic provinces (Blair 1950). The biotic provinces (from the perspective of Brantley Reservoir) extend to the eastern edges of the Llano Estacado (Kansan) to the northwest through the western flank of the Pecos Valley (Navahonian) and form a broadening funnel flanking the Pecos to the south (Chihuahuan).

Vegetation Studies

Prehistoric human populations within each of these provinces would be influenced by distribution of biotic resources. Bailey (1928) inventoried some of the important animal resources of the Carlsbad Caverns vicinity. However, much of the information on the distribution and habits of these animals is too general to be of use in specifying microhabitats. A few quantitative distributional studies of plants have been done in the Chihuahuan Province (Gehlbach 1967; Gardner 1950). In addition, some specifically ethnobotanical work has been done in the region (Castetter and Opler 1936). Basehart

(1960) provides an excellent catalog of the more important plant and animal resources of the Mescalero Apache who occupied the Middle Pecos drainage and roamed widely in this area historically. The seasonal use and general physiographic range in which these foods were obtained by the Mescalero is presented in Fig. 3.

Evidence of Shifts in Elevational and Zonational Tolerances of Vegetation

Because no inventory or quantitative studies have been done of the Brantley Reservoir flora and fauna, it is difficult to confirm the existence of more specific life zones within the project area. Gehlbach (1967) is able to show that different plant species have remarkably different soil, temperature, elevation, and exposure tolerances in the southern Guadalupe Mountains. For example, *Agave lecheguilla* (mescal), a primary foodstuff for the Mescalero, is dominant between 4,220 to 4,800 ft in the southern Guadalupe Mountains; it is semidominant between 3,700 to 5,200 ft but completely absent from sample quadrants above or below these elevations (Gehlbach 1967: 410). Of the aboriginally important economic plants listed in Fig. 3, only datil, sotol, mesquite, and prickly pear were noted in the Seven Rivers area; only mesquite occurs in sufficient quantities today to be a major foodstuff. However, a slight shift in environmental conditions might change these distributions significantly. Harris (1970) and Murray (1957) show that a major climatic shift occurred about 15,000 years ago. This shift may have raised the life zones apparent today as much as 4,000 ft reflecting a gradual desiccation of the environment between 15,000 and 7000 B.P. The magnitude of this shift is based on slim evidence; it should be more carefully studied for its temporal parameters, location of occurrence, and associated faunal and floral assemblages. Shifts of far less magnitude easily could have

changed the food potential of the Seven Rivers area for prehistoric peoples.

Vegetation Resource Zones

The fauna and flora of the Pecos Basin are conveniently divided here into lowland, midland, and highland associations. This simplification of the biotic cross section in the Pecos Basin was devised as a tool to place plant and animal communities in a generalized framework for ethnographic reconstruction. The behavior of the flora of the Pecos Basin has been much more carefully investigated than has the behavior of fauna with respect to geographic ranges and habits. Little is known of the habits of game animals with respect to the seasonal or geographic distributions of populations. However, recent studies of deer behavior (Wood et. al. 1970) indicate the potential of detailed wildlife studies to the interpretation of archaeological remains.

The highlands area is recognized as the mountainous zone of the western flank of the Pecos Basin. This zone extends down to about 5,000 ft into the Piñon and Juniper Woodlands. Empirically, this area can be distinguished by a general steep topographic gradient. The midland has been distinguished geologically by Hayes (1964). This zone corresponds in the Roswell Basin with the broad flank of the Diamond A pediment paralleling the Sacramento Mountains. Here is an area of broken topography and generally gradual downward slope to the east. Juniper, desert shrub, and grasslands characterize the flora of this zone. The lowland area roughly encompasses the flanks of the Pecos River. This is a scrub-and-grass community dominated largely by alluvial deposits, gentle slope, and shifting sands. It extends to the east where there are numerous subsidence basins, wide gypsum plains, and eventually the caprock of the Llano Estacado. The Seven Rivers area falls within the lowland vegetation zone.

The reality of these divisions should be

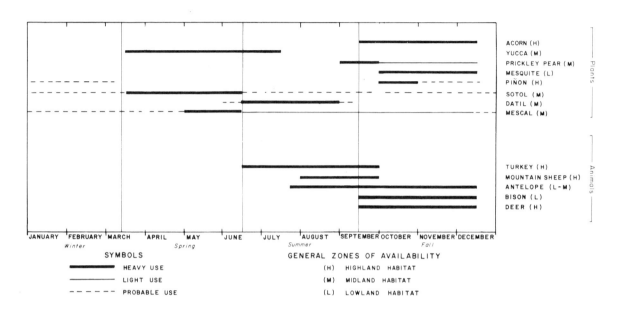

FIG. 3–Periods of Use of Plants and Animals by the Mescalero Apache.

verified by quantitative distributional studies. Careful studies of soils, current vegetation, and palynology would help to reconstruct the details of the environmental changes that have taken place in the thousands of years that man has utilized the Seven Rivers area as well as help to test the reality of the structural divisions proposed here.

ARCHAEOLOGICAL EVIDENCE AND ENVIRONMENTAL RECONSTRUCTION IN THE MIDDLE PECOS

METHODS OF MEASURING PAST ENVIRONMENTAL CONDITIONS

More detailed studies of changes in the environment are needed. A radical change like the virtual destruction of grama grass plains and replacement by mesquite and creosote bush as suggested for the last 100 years would have definite ramifications for the fauna and human potential of the Seven Rivers area (see "Anglo-American Archaeology of the Seven Rivers Area," later in text). Information from environmental and archaeological studies in surrounding areas is compiled here to demonstrate the feasibility of more intensive study. It is suggested that a major untested theory about prehistoric population shifts *can* be tested with more thorough environmental data.

Jelinek (1967: 130-64), Duffield (1970), and Dillehay (1975) have suggested relatively recent and widespread environmental changes which have affected critical food/animal distributions and human populations in the southern plains. Palynological and faunal studies independently corroborate some of these changes; however, this corroboration is largely in the realm of how the interpreter organized the information. Thus, Martin (1967) interprets the pollen record from a site in the Middle Pecos as being largely anthropogenic while Jelinek (1967: 134-39) interprets this same record as evidence of climatic change causing a shift in floral and faunal communities.

Pollen (Hafsten 1961) and dendrological studies (Schulman 1956) conducted independently of archaeological contexts in the Middle Pecos drainage give sketchy support to portions of each of the models of environmental change in the last 10,000 years in the Pecos drainage. These data and the indirect information on the environment contained in previous archaeological work can be used to synthesize a model of climatic fluctuation. At this time, extrapolation from dated archaeological contexts in other regions and dated diagnostic artifact types are the only way to order archaeological materials from the Middle Pecos region to correlate with the environmental model to be presented. Archaeological techniques are available now so that future work should not only date archaeological contexts but also provide needed environmental information.

ARCHAEOLOGICAL PERIODS AND ENVIRONMENTS

The Paleo-Indian Period and Environment (12,000 to 7000 B.P.)

Excavations specifically aimed at locating the earliest human inhabitants of North America were conducted some time ago in the Middle Pecos drainage (Howard 1930, 1935). Quantitative data that can be used in reconstructing the environmental conditions were not compiled in this early work. Palynology and sampling techniques for vegetal and faunal materials were unknown sources of data for archaeologists working in the Middle Pecos. Although considerable attention was paid to the compilation of the inventory of faunal remains from these excavations, provenience and dating generally were unclear. Controlled sampling was not used.

Some of this early work in the Guadalupe Mountains produces evidence bearing on environmental conditions. Two excavations have since produced radiocarbon dates; both

13

of these dates confirm occupation and human deposition of early materials.

Burnet Cave (Howard 1930, 1935; Burns 1967: 19-25) is locally the most famous Paleo-Indian site. Information about the faunal assemblage from this site is more complete than from any other early excavations in the Middle Pecos Region—such as those of Ayer (1936) at William's Cave and Mera (1938) from several caves in the Guadalupe Mountains. About one-third of the assemblage consists of rodents and small mammals and probably reflects the microhabitat of any given rockshelter in the region. Another third of the identified faunal remains are horse, musk-ox, and other extinct species (Murray 1957). A large portion of the remaining third of the fauna include deer, scavengers, predators, foxes, bobcats, cougars, and raptorial birds that used the cave (Schultz and Howard 1935). Also in the cave deposits associated with the fauna are artifacts including a "Folsom style" projectile point. The presence of extinct fauna (about one-third of the 212 identifiable bones) suggests that the cave was used by animals before early man's tools and refuse were deposited in the cave. Burns (1967: 40) reports a recent radiocarbon date of 7432 ± 300 B.P. from the cave deposits, but the precise stratigraphic relationship of the sample to either the extinct fauna or the Folsom projectile is uncertain.

Excavations at Burnet Cave apparently stimulated additional search for cave materials with extinct fauna in the Guadalupe Mountains. The assemblage of fauna reported by Ayer (1936) from William's Cave contained little extinct fauna (6 identified horse elements); and although archaeological evidence of human occupation was found, there was no temporally diagnostic material reported. The only other possibly early faunal remains with human associations were reported by Mera (1938). However, the artifactual materials (10 pieces of extinct horse bone) from the series of shelters which Mera excavated can only be assigned to a time period by bracketing. No diagnostic Paleo-Indian points were recovered, and limited numbers of ceramics occurred above the major levels in which the horse bones appeared (Mera 1938). Several more recent excavations in caves in the Guadalupe Mountains have yielded extinct fauna but no early human occupation (Harris 1970).

Excavations at Hermit's Cave (Ferdon 1946) also have yielded a radiocarbon date (obtained subsequent to the publication of the report) in association with human remains. Unfortunately, Ferdon does not report the recovery of faunal remains, and no diagnostic Paleo-Indian materials were recovered. The stratigraphy is better documented than in any of the excavations so far undertaken in the area although rodent disturbance in the cave deposits is a major problem in stratigraphic interpretation. A few potsherds found in the upper levels give an upper bracket for the occupation. Recently, radiocarbon dates were run on charcoal of known provenience. The material rested on basal deposits in the cave and cannot be correlated, except by its burned character, to human activity. The dates are rather anomalous, averaging about 12,500 B.P. (Haynes 1967: 269).

Based on these reports it is difficult to say with confidence much about early man's relation to his environment in the Guadalupe Mountains. It seems that the area was supporting a range of now extinct fauna contemporaneous with early human occupation of the area. The presence of horse in all reported samples may indicate the existence of a grassland environment even in the steep canyons of the Guadalupe Mountains where the archaeological sites with the earliest materials are located.

More recent excavations in the Middle Pecos region have tended to confirm the existence of a Paleo-Indian occupation on the plains east of the Pecos but add little to empirical evidence about subsistence. At the Rattlesnake Draw Site (Smith, East-Smith, and

Runyan 1966), parallel-flaked points were found in association with wash deposits and possibly some alluvial redeposition of materials. A little farther afield is the Milnesand bison kill at which parallel-flaked points were found but from which radiocarbon dates are unreported (Sellards 1955; Warnica and Williamson 1968). Conditions in these two sites can be compared most reasonably to those at Blackwater Draw and the Clovis Site itself. However, no faunal material (except bison at Milnesand) or stratigraphic and palynological evidence are currently available for environmental reconstruction from the Milnesand or Rattlesnake Draw localities. Archaeological survey in the Brantley Reservoir has located diagnostic artifacts assignable to both the fluted point and parallel-flaked projectile traditions, but so far no paleoclimatic data for these occupations are available.

Climatic Conditions

For the reconstruction of the environment of the Seven Rivers area at this early period, data gathered at Blackwater Draw to the north and a number of sites at the mouth of the Pecos in Val Verde County, Texas must be relied upon. This requires an expedition well beyond the Middle Pecos boundaries for such information, and a derived environmental model which can be more specifically applied to the Seven Rivers area may be produced as the result of future excavation in the Middle Pecos.

Many discussions of geoclimatic and environmental events in northwestern America cite a model of climatic change proposed by Ernst Antevs (1955). This model has not formalized the *explanation* for a series of proposed climatic changes in the arid western United States. The model does propose a general desiccation and retreat of pluvial and glacial climates to more northern latitudes between approximately 11,000 and 5,000 years ago. This resulted in an exceptionally

dry climate (Altithermal period) between 7500 and 4000 B.P. (Antevs 1955: 323) after which climatic conditions became somewhat moister and resembled today's climate and conditions. In addition several more recent droughts were suggested by Antevs, but these may be confined to more restricted regions. The "Long Drought" or Altithermal seems to be reflected in measurable changes in the climatic and environmental record over much of North America. Bryant (1969: 116-29), in his synthesis of the west Texas environmental record, suggests that the climatic conditions up to about 2500 B.P. corresponded closely to the Antevs model including a more recent fluctuation toward a mesic environment after 2900 B.P.

Even though Hafsten (1961: 82) is cautious in assuming the pollen samples on the Wolf Creek Ranch on the Peñasco River are representative, Bryant (1969: 127-28) uses this pollen locality as further confirmation of the general sequence of events in west Texas. Palynological evidence appears to support the Antevs model in southeastern New Mexico up to and including the "Fairbank Drought" between 2500 and 3000 B.P. Archaeological evidence alone also seems to corroborate the finding of a more mesic environment at 2500 B.P. (Dillehay 1975).

Interpretations of geological evidence for these climatic fluctuations are somewhat less consistent, especially with regard to the "Fairbank Drought." At Blackwater Draw, Haynes's data suggest a general confirmation of Altithermal conditions with geological events. He also correlates the Altithermal with geological events near Midland and at Rich Lake further to the east on the Llano Estacado (Haynes 1975: 76-77). Miller's alluvial chronology also can be interpolated to fit Antevs's climatic model (Martin 1963: 62-64; Miller 1958).

The factors affecting geological and climatic events in the Middle Pecos Valley are similar to those in surrounding areas. There is some evidence for the existence of an increasingly dry climate with more xeric vegetation and a probable disappearance of bison from the Middle Pecos Valley and surrounding areas starting about 7000 B.P. The thermal maximum occurred at about 5500 B.P. (Antevs 1955).

Changes in the animal *and* plant resources during the Altithermal necessitated readjustment of the human exploitative system if not more drastic and measurable changes in technological and settlement systems. While water itself may not have become a direct critical factor to small human populations, the distribution of animals and plants with respect to moisture may have some explanatory value in the human adjustment. There is no evidence from the Llano Estacado or the Pecos region that the location of major sources of surface water changed drastically. Large herbivores might for instance be insensitive to direct surface water changes but sensitive to moisture levels as they affect plant communities. In fact, the herbivores may have needed very little surface water in the immediate grazing environment but only an accessibility to water within a certain distance from the grazing area (Judge 1973: 332-33).

Conjectural Conditions

The Altithermal conditions suggest an increase in seasonal evaporation of water sources that may have already been ephemeral. On the other hand, streams and springs in the Pecos Valley probably were consistent and relatively permanent. Overgrazing and reduction in general atmospheric moisture levels may have severely limited the herbivorous carrying capacity of the area. This same decrease in moisture may have forced many plants used by people for food into smaller areas or different areas having the same general effect of increasing the distance between traditionally utilized plant food resource areas. If this is true, the Altithermal may have

caused major readjustment of lifestyles, if not abandonment of the area, and at least an initial decrease in the human population of the Middle Pecos. This may, in part, explain the lack of evidence for human occupation in the Middle Pecos during the early and middle Archaic.

The Archaic Period and Environment
(7000 to 1000 B.P.)

As in most areas of the Southwest, the Archaic in the Middle Pecos is poorly understood. Radiocarbon dates for Archaic sites are nonexistent in the Middle Pecos drainage with the exception of those reported by Applegarth (1975). For this reason, it is difficult to reconstruct environmental conditions in conjunction with cultural materials. The Archaic period in the Middle Pecos area is largely a hypothetical one, resting on evidence no better than the existence of a temporal gap of cultural associations and some very slim stylistic analogies with other areas where the Archaic materials are dated by radiocarbon methods. Although we lack good evidence for human adaptation in the Middle Pecos during the Archaic, paleoenvironmental information independent of archaeological contexts from this period from near the Seven Rivers area is available.

Several caves in the Guadalupe and Sacramento Mountains may contain occupational debris from the 5000 to 2000 B.P. time interval. Hermit's Cave is one of these (Ferdon 1946). Mera (1938) also excavated in a number of caves that might have occupations attributable to this period. A similar artifact assemblage to many of Mera's "cave" assemblages comes from Fresnal Shelter in the Sacramento Mountains. This site has at least one radiocarbon date in the Archaic time range at 3615 ± 120 years B.P. (Human Systems Research 1972: 21). Preliminary and programmatic statements have been released from this important excavation, and the results provide a model of excellence for other archaeological work in the area. Preliminary faunal analysis suggests dependence on deer, which occur in a ratio of almost 12:1 deer bones to all other vertebrate remains identifiable from the cave. More recent evidence suggests that rodents may have been a secondarily important food resource as indicated by the numbers of burned fragments found in association with hearths (Human Systems Research 1973: 398-401). The faunal assemblage includes fauna of only the recent geologic period and represents specifically human use and discard patterns more certainly than does any excavated faunal assemblage from the southeastern quarter of New Mexico.

Data on utilization of floral species have not been published as unambiguously as has the faunal material from Fresnal Shelter. A complete and quantitative report is awaited with great interest. Information provided does suggest an extensive use of local resources and also provides interesting archaeological data on species and availability (Human Systems Research 1972: 189-218). Inspection would suggest that the plant inventory alone could represent a continuous all-year occupation of the shelter. The ability to store and preserve seasonally edible portions of fruiting plants makes these plants more available, and so their remains may be present even at sites used when the fruits are not naturally procurable.

Recent cave excavations by Riches (1970) in the Guadalupe Mountains suggest that a subsistence system similar to that of Fresnal Shelter may have existed during the Archaic on the eastern slopes of the Guadalupe Mountains. Radiocarbon samples from the middle strata at Honest Injun Cave date cultural material at 2930 B.P. (Applegarth 1975). The possible presence of cultural boundaries make similarities between archaeological settlements from the eastern Guadalupe Mountains and undated settlements from the western Sacramento Mountains unclear. Certainly a

comparison of these materials would aid immeasurably in controlling for paleoenvironmental differences in these locations. A pollen profile is available from one excavated shelter (Riches 1970). Until more complete chronological information is available, the pollen profile cannot be fitted well into the Antevs model. A peak in *Graminae* pollen in the 9-15 inch level of Honest Injun Cave (Riches 1970: 109) correlates with either one of two peaks in nonarboreal pollen suggested in Hafsten's (1961) pollen profile from Wolf Creek Ranch on the Peñasco River.

Perhaps more relevant to the archaeology of the Seven Rivers area in terms of ecological setting is a survey at Andrews Lake (Collins 1968). This is an area that contrasts markedly with the Guadalupe or Sacramento Mountain environments of many of the sites discussed thus far. It is nearly as close to Seven Rivers as the Fresnal Shelter excavations but in the opposite direction. Andrews Lake is on the southern border of the Llano Estacado. Salt cedar, grama, mesquite, prickly pear, and yucca are the current vegetation dominants (Collins 1968: 39). Collins (1968: 5;138-52) recognizes the existence of a late Archaic occupation in the area on the basis of projectile point styles. However, relatively recent historic or protohistoric sites were the subject of excavation. The current environment of "Archaic sites" located in the survey are similar in deposition and exposure to sites at Brantley Reservoir. Collins (1968: 40-45) attempts to make inferences about the climate and paleoenvironmental sequence for the Holocene, but new data are related only to the late Ceramic components and are discussed later in this report.

Pre-Ceramic associations are also suggested by Jelinek (1967) in his survey of the Middle Pecos. He reports Archaic materials defined on the basis of seriation of projectile points and comparison with material from other areas, especially Texas. However, no Archaic sites were excavated nor were further detailed studies done on Archaic materials. The pollen profile presented by Jelinek does not extend to pre-Ceramic times.

A recent publication on the paleoecology of the Blackwater Draw does not include analysis of data collected for the post-Paleo-Indian period (Wendorf and Hester 1975). Recent excavations near Blackwater Draw have been aimed at the Archaic and subsequent occupation of the area, but faunal analysis and pollen data are not available (Kunz 1969; Kunz, Gamache, and Agogino 1973).

Paleoenvironmental reconstruction for the Archaic period in the Middle Pecos is difficult. Despite the long interest in Archaic occupation in west Texas and eastern New Mexico [as evidenced by Cosgrove's Hueco Cave Dweller Period span (1947), Mera's (1938) excavations, and Bradley's (1959) preliminary report on a possible Archaic site in Carlsbad Caverns National Park], too few dated contexts are available.

However, further environmental data are available. In conjunction with an extended multidisciplinary study of the Llano Estacado (Wendorf 1961), Hafsten has built a pollen sequence for the Wolf Ranch Canyon of the Peñasco River. This information has been scaled with the one radiocarbon date on this profile and interpolated back to about 4500 B.P. (Hafsten 1961: 72; see fig. 4, this volume).

An application of this scaled pollen profile to the Archaic period shows generally moderate amounts of arboreal pollen present at the Wolf Creek Ranch locality. There is a minor drop in arboreal pollen about 3500 B.P. and a somewhat more marked drop accompanied by a subsequent sharp rise at 2800 to 2900 B.P. This profile forms part of the basis of Bryant's suggestion (1969: 127-28) that a sharp rise in arboreal pollen is correlated with more mesic conditions throughout southern New Mexico and west Texas. Temporally the xeric conditions which preceded this can be correlated with Antevs's "Fair-

bank Drought" (Antevs 1955: 329). The fact that the Fairbank Drought appears to be just slightly later (close to 2500 B.P., the mesic period of Bryant) is attributable to slight inaccuracies in dating and correlation of events in different regions. This general correlation should not be visualized as the actual end and beginning points of mesic or xeric conditions but actually should be viewed, at this point, as periods of some unspecified but clearly evident climatic fluctuation. The continued reference to xeric and mesic conditions is a reflection of the lack of other suitable terminology.

Another reversal to "xeric conditions" is apparent on the scaled pollen profile in the low arboreal pollen count about 1500 B.P. This correlates rather well with Antevs's (1955) "Whitewater Drought." The increasingly "mesic conditions" after this period signal the beginning of Basketmaker occupation in the "central" Southwest and the end of the Archaic. The "Archaic lifeway" is visualized as continuing until about 1000 B.P. in the Middle Pecos. Although the available evidence for postulating the nature of the Archaic subsistence system in the Middle Pecos is limited, it is sufficient for the formulation of a model of human response to these changing conditions.

Paleoclimatically, the Archaic seems to have begun and ended with severe "xeric conditions." During the intervening period, there were some general small-scale climatic fluctuations with short-lived dry conditions about 2700 or 2800 B.P. and succeeding mesic conditions in the entire southeast New Mexico—west Texas area by about 2500 B.P. Subsistence in the west slope of the Sacramento Mountains (Fresnal Shelter) about 3000 B.P. was dependent on large numbers of deer and small mammals (rodents) and unknown quantities of plant foods. Conditions at the mouth of the Pecos were probably somewhat different, and Dibble (1968: 75) has suggested that bison were rare in the area. Occasionally,

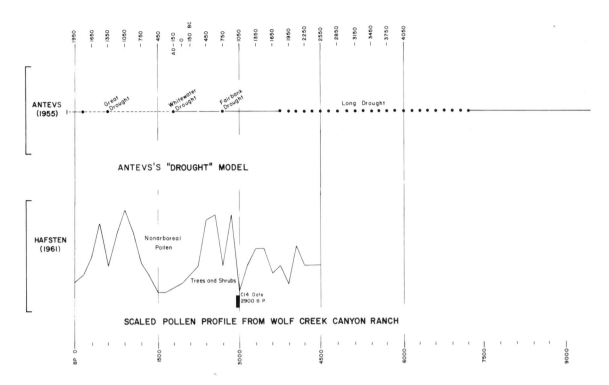

FIG. 4–Correlation of Paleoclimatic Models.

he suggests, herds were pursued into the Lower Pecos region by bison-dependent people generally restricted to the Plains. When conditions allowed the bison to move south, parts of this human population would follow. Certainly the Middle Pecos supported herds of bison occasionally entering the area. But the archaeological evidence presented above shows that subsistence during the Archaic was more dependent on deer, rodents, and plant foods than on bison in the Middle Pecos area. Evidence from Fresnal Shelter indicates this; the high proportion of rodents and deer in Mera's limited faunal analysis also is supportive (Mera 1938: 48-49). Archaeologically, such conditions should be represented by evidence of intermittent use of bison during the Archaic in the Middle Pecos. Considering the supposed infrequent occurrence of bison in the area, it is expected that campsites are located with respect to resources that do not necessarily match the locations of a bison habitat.

The Ceramic Period and Environment (1000 to 400 B.P.)

Ceramics of the Middle Pecos Valley are known to have been manufactured as early as A.D. 900. Ceramic sites in the Middle Pecos are quite numerous; 30 of the prehistoric sites located within Brantley Reservoir contain ceramics. Some authors have preferred to label sites in this area that have ceramics on them as "Jornada" sites (Corley 1965). However, this assumes: (1) that ethnic and cultural affiliations of the Seven Rivers area sites and others on the Pecos and the Llano Estacado are known, or (2) that the sites in these areas are indistinguishable from sites in the Tularosa Basin or the El Paso area that have similar ceramic types. Until the nature of this affiliation can be more substantially confirmed, the more neutral term "Ceramic" should be used.

Ceramics occur in many of the shelters in the Guadalupe Mountains mentioned above

(Mera 1938; Riches 1970; Ferdon 1946). Knowledge of the artifact inventory of open ceramic sites is also comparatively extensive. Palynological, faunal, and geological evidence from which to reconstruct environmental conditions is minimal.

Six archaeological surveys in the areas in and surrounding the Middle Pecos provide some basis on which to infer ecological conditions (J. Runyan, personal communication). The Lea County Archeological Society survey of Lea County and the Texas Archeological Society survey of the Guadalupe Mountains National Park (Shafer 1970) are important for a broad-scale appreciation of the nature of archaeological remains present. Ceramics are found in contexts ranging from dispersed scatters of artifacts and burned rock to association with burned rock mounds and ring middens (Shafer 1970; Leslie 1965; Phelps 1974). A third survey even further to the south near Sierra Blanca, Texas is characterized by similar remains in open sites and small rockshelters (Skinner, Steed, and Bearden 1974). A reconnaissance in the same general area near Van Horn, Texas yielded small numbers of sherds in very small (generally less than 1,000 sq m) sites (Skinner and Bousman 1973). During the latter part of the Ceramic period (about A.D. 1400) south of Seven Rivers, roofed structures are reported by the Lea County Archeological Society survey and at the Andrews Lake locality (Collins 1968; Leslie 1965, 1968; Runyan 1972). These sites have a characteristic late pottery type known as Ochoa Brown. A survey of Carlsbad Caverns National Park provides a series of dates for ring midden use between about A.D. 1100 and 1500 (Greer 1968b; Sommer 1968). Some dates from burned rock mounds are as early as A.D. 800, but most are in the A.D. 900s with a mean of about A.D. 950. A midden circle in Crockett County had no ceramics in association (Sommer 1968), while one near El Paso had a full range of Chupadero B/W, El Paso Brown, El Paso Poly-chrome, and Playas Red (Greer 1968b), perhaps suggesting that the radiocarbon samples and the pottery deposition were at different times.

The one extensive archaeological survey and excavation to the north of Seven Rivers shows an assemblage of remains quite different from those to the south. Near Fort Sumner, Jelinek (1967) located several sites with shallow circular pit rooms and ceramic assemblages with strong affiliations to Rio Grande Anasazi culture. Relatively frequent occurrences of Red Mesa B/W and Cebolleta B/W characterize this area. Occasional occurrences of Lino Gray, Socorro B/W, and Santa Fe B/W in Jelinek's (1967: 60) survey area are rare or absent types south of the Seven Rivers.

The report on almost a decade of excavations in the Sierra Blanca region confirms the existence of a rather heavy pithouse and Puebloan occupation of the Sacramento Mountains and the upper reaches of the Diamond A pediment. This later occupation can legitimately be called Jornada in nature (Kelley 1966). The similarities of this previously little studied area with remains in the Tularosa Basin and the Jornada del Muerto is rather remarkable (Marshall 1973). Excavation in the Upper Peñasco drainage in the 1930s by Jennings (1940) are the closest reported Jornada type assemblages to the Seven Rivers area. The structures and the assemblages of these sites are placed into the Glencoe Phase by Kelley (1966: 59). Other excavations in this area confirm the Jornada nature of the late prehistoric occupation of the midlands and highlands of the Middle Pecos (Green 1956). On the other hand, a unit pueblo near Roswell on the Hondo Drainage, known as Bloom Mound, is a representative of the Jornada culture quite near the Pecos River. This site has a complex of materials that is unrepresented in any known sites further south in the Pecos drainage (Ross 1969; Kelley 1966; Burns 1967). The evidence for a cultural boundary between Jornada and Middle Pecos peoples is slim; the nature of the boundary is certainly in question. Whether it represents an alternate adaptive strategy of a single *cultunit* (Naroll 1964, 1973) or whether two distinctive cultunits are involved is uncertain. This must rest on further archaeological work to test the hypothesis that the two areas are culturally continuous.

Further excavated materials for paleoecological study to contrast the Northern Pecos and Middle Pecos are limited to Jelinek's survey near Fort Sumner and to the pollen profile from Wolf Canyon. No contemporary paleoecological material exists for the Ceramic period south of Roswell in the Pecos Valley system until near the mouth of the river at Amistad Reservoir. One possible exception is material from the Salt Cedar Site (Collins 1968: 189; Bryant 1969: 77-79), which has an archaeological context that is considered later in this report. The material from the mouth of the Pecos is too far removed to thoroughly judge its relevance to the last 1,000 years in the Middle Pecos (Bryant 1969: 128-29).

Jelinek (1967), Collins (1968), Duffield (1970), and Dillehay (1975) all suggest evidence for rather marked economic change in the Southern Plains and the fringes of the Llano Estacado at about A.D. 1300. Whether this change is generated by actual climatic fluctuations is undetermined. This evidence for change consists of changes in projectile point styles (Jelinek 1967: 152-60), pottery styles (Jelinek 1967; Collins 1968; Leslie 1965; Runyan 1972), the presence of variant habitation styles (Jelinek 1967), and the increase of bison remains in archaeological contexts (Jelinek 1967; Duffield 1970; Dillehay 1975; Collins 1968). The cultural significance of this change is uncertain. Duffield (1970) and Dillehay (1975) suggest that it may be actual expansion or shifting of Central Plains peoples into more favorable bison ranges as a response to ecological and climatological

changes at this time. This is in contrast to the pattern suggested by Dibble (1968) discussed for the Archaic in an earlier section of this report. This Ceramic period infusion of people seems to be tied to a more diverse and flexible economy than the earlier one. The extent of involvement of these changes during the late Ceramic period in the Seven Rivers area is completely unknown. The suggested paleoecological cause of the change in surrounding areas is reflected in some limited palynological and zoological materials from the Middle Pecos. Regarding this change, there are large quantities of bison remains from the Late McKenzie Phase near Fort Sumner (Jelinek 1967: 137) and at the Salt Cedar Site (Collins 1968: 118) which are unknown from earlier periods in these areas.

Jelinek presents data from near Fort Sumner that show no great variation in pollen profile from about A.D. 1000 to 1300, except for an increase in grass pollen at the end of the sequence. Jelinek (1967: 134) interprets this as a change in the regional botanical picture whereas Martin (1967: 134) cautions that this may only reflect an on-the-spot change due to the ecology of human occupational patterns.

Hafsten's (1961) profile from Wolf Creek suffers from different depositional ambiguities. When scaled to the "Ceramic" period, it shows one major fluctuation: a reduction of arboreal pollen at A.D. 1350 or 1400. This is reflected by an increase in *Graminae*, *Chenopodiaceae*, and *Artemisia*, and a reduction of *Compositae* (Hafsten 1961: fig. 27). Jelinek's data from the Middle Pecos shows a decrease in *both* composites and chenopods. The pollen data then show some consistency in a rise of grass pollen between A.D. 1300 and 1400. Otherwise, Hafsten's information shows the maximum arboreal pollen for his whole sequence at A.D. 1050. This by itself is little evidence to hypothesize actual changes in subsistence between the Archaic and the Ceramic periods.

Jelinek shows the presence of *Zea* pollen in small quantities throughout the sequence; there is no *Zea* pollen reported in the pollen samples at the Salt Cedar site (Collins 1968: 189). Kelley (1966: 187-90) finds direct evidence of maize in the puebloan Sierra Blanca area. Pollen samples from Honest Injun Cave near Carlsbad (Riches 1970), probably of late Archaic age, however show no *Zea* pollen.

The large number of bison bones from the Middle Pecos at a site near Fort Sumner (Jelinek 1967) and from the Salt Cedar site do not fully establish the late Ceramic period subsistence picture (Collins 1968). Rabbits are the second most significant fauna in the Middle Pecos assemblage (Jelinek 1967: 137). Very small numbers of deer and antelope are represented. Conversely, Collins (1968: 116) finds that rabbits are represented in counts only after bison, antelope, and deer, in that order. The small sample sizes limit interpretation. Perhaps rodents suffered a decreasing importance for food in the later part of the Ceramic period as a result of availability of larger game. The suggested high dependence on deer in the Archaic turning to bison in the late Ceramic may be due entirely to sample bias at the locations of excavation materials. Unpublished faunal information from Billy the Kid Cave would make a stronger argument possible (Kunz 1969; Kunz, Gamache, and Agogino 1973).

Before leaving the prehistoric cultures of the Middle Pecos it would be well to see if Antevs's (1955) model of climatic fluctuation suggested for the west can fit the data available in the area of the Pecos Valley during the Ceramic period. The maximum of *Graminae* suggested in the pollen at Wolf Creek Ranch Canyon and near Fort Sumner corresponds quite well with what Antevs labelled as the "Great Drought" for the Western United States. If these climatic events can be correlated, the "drought" on the Pueblo Plateau does not seem to have the same implications as the grass maximum had in the Pecos Val-

ley. This difference may in itself be due to the different environmental situation and cultural potentials of the Pecos Valley peoples as opposed to the agricultural potentials of which the Jornada are a part.

The Historic Aboriginal
Period and Environment
(400 to 100 B.P.)

Little is known about the transition from prehistory to history on the Pecos. Early Spanish documents (for instance, the journal of De Sosa) are not clear accounts for ethnographic purposes (Bolton 1963). The myriad of names that were applied to groups of natives make the descriptions very difficult to interpret. A great deal of scholarly effort has been expended on relating the ethnographic descriptions of the Spanish to groups that are recognizable today in southeastern New Mexico and western Texas. The controversies surrounding these problems well can be appreciated in any of the following sources: Basehart (1960: 121-23); Schroeder (1973: 124-44); Jelinek (1967: 18-23); Harrington (1940); and Opler and Opler (1950). Detailed analysis of the various historical events reputed to have taken place in the Middle Pecos is necessary in the future. Such an enterprise would be of great value in reconstructing climatic conditions.

Archaeologically, very little is known of the historic occupation in the area. Burns (1972) has prepared prolegomenon to such research with reference to historic Indian campsites. The closest historically documented aboriginal sites which extend into prehistoric times are Gran Quivira (Vivian 1961) and Pecos Pueblo (Kidder 1924: 61-87). Indirect evidence of the presence of historic aboriginal sites in the Middle Pecos is available. Metal projectile points occur as surface finds in the area. Mera (1938: 23-24) diagrams a site of "stone circles" in the Guadalupe Mountains. These appear to be similar to the tipi ring sites recorded on the Canadian River (Hammack 1965), presumably of historic age. Schroeder (1965) has excavated a shelter in the Guadalupe Mountains with historic Indian materials, and a complete report is forthcoming. It is almost certain that there were people in the Pecos Valley continuously throughout this period, and the most probable modern representatives of the major occupants are the Mescalero Apache (Basehart 1960). Unfortunately, no archaeology was undertaken in conjunction with Mescalero Land Claims in the 1960s when ethnographic and ethnohistoric research was undertaken. As pointed out previously, excellent information on Mescalero subsistence patterns is available; and development of these patterns into a consistent explanatory model is the subject of a later section of this paper. There is some evidence of changing climatic conditions over the last 400 years from nonarchaeological sources.

The Wolf Creek Canyon Ranch pollen sequence shows a steady decline in arboreal pollen over the last 450 years. Today arboreal pollen has reached a very low level in the area. Another potential source of climatic information is the tree ring indices collected from the Guadalupe and Sacramento Mountains (Schulman 1956: 117). Plotting the 10-year means of the growth index shows a widely varying fluctuation about the mean growth (fig. 5). The record, starting at A.D. 1665, indicates that in this time span there are two long-term periods of low tree growth (drought?). The first is between A.D. 1665 and 1680, the second between A.D. 1865 and 1880. The second low growth period correlated well with general drought periods recorded in the central and northern Rio Grande in New Mexico (Zubrow 1974: 11). This second period also predates drought conditions mentioned in historical accounts (see "Anglo-American Archaeology of the Seven Rivers Area" later in text) and corresponds almost precisely to the initial Anglo settlement of the Pecos Val-

ley and to the movement of vast herds of cattle up the Pecos starting about A.D. 1869. At this time the grasslands along the Pecos are described as dense short grass prairies by travelers (Keleher 1959: ix-x).

The Anglo-American Period and Environment (100 B.P. to Present)

No published archaeological work has been accomplished at Anglo-American sites in the Pecos Valley although excavations have been carried out at Fort Sumner (Wilson 1968). Whether climatic conditions can be tied to changes in settlement patterns, population, or subsistence during this period is unclear. Several important changes in economic systems argue against direct correlations of climate and social process in the recent historic period. Irrigation, artesian and nonartesian wells, and conservation measures tend to change the nature of the mechanisms of adaptation. Rainfall records exist for Carlsbad starting in A.D. 1895; these show an average annual precipitation of about 13 inches of rain per year. However, this has fluctuated from less than 3 inches to more than 33 inches of rain in individual years (U. S. Department of Commerce 1971). It has been suggested above that radical changes have taken place in the biotic regime in the Pecos Valley in the Anglo period. Much more information exists on this period than any other for climatic conditions and ecological relationships. Unfortunately, the kind of information usually is not similar to that available from paleoclimatic sequences. Palynological studies of modern pollen distribution are rare. Studies of actual animal distribution and abundance are also comparatively rare. This provides no control for paleoclimatic data which makes reconstruction even more hazardous.

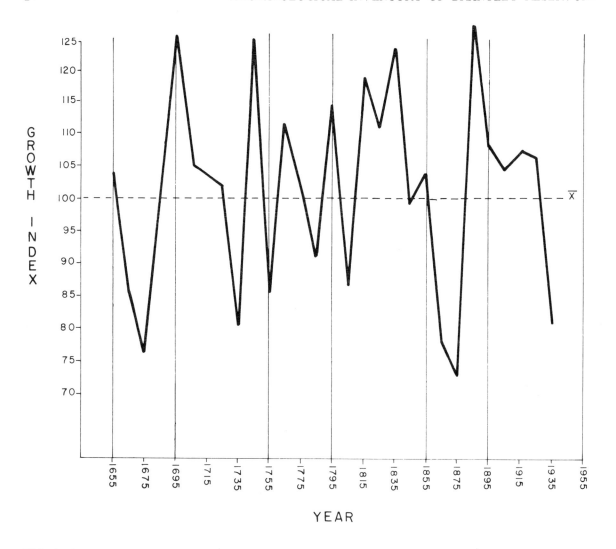

FIG. 5—Growth of Trees in the Guadalupe Mountains from A.D. 1655 to A.D. 1935. Ten-year averages of the Growth Index were calculated for this chart.. (Data from Shulman 1956.)

MODERN POLLEN RAIN IN THE MIDDLE PECOS

Pollen sampling of modern soils has been done recently by several investigators in the Middle Pecos region. This information is synthesized here to try to obtain a picture of what pollen reflects in terms of the present environment. It sets the stage for developing a subsistence model which takes into account the interrelationships of environmental and cultural factors in the Middle Pecos. This is a rough approximation which can be refined by future studies. Pollen samples are a valuable tool if they can be used to establish differences in the distribution of modern and prehistoric plant communities. The current vegetation pattern in the Pecos Basin is presented in Table 1.

Soil samples of pollen collected in the Pecos Basin as representative of botanical distribution on the site of collection are difficult to interpret. Bryant (1969:97) collected several samples in an oak-juniper savannah at the southern tip of the Guadalupe Mountains. Examination of the sample shows that over 50% of one and 75% of another is pine pollen.

TABLE 1*
Vegetation Zones in the Middle Pecos Area

TYPE	DOMINANT VEGETATION	ACREAGE (in 1,000s)	PERCENTAGE OF WATERSHED
Short Grass	Grasses	7,132	30
Desert	Grasses, Cheno-Ams	4,258	18
Southern Desert Shrub	Composites, Grasses, Cheno-Ams	7,200	30
Tall Grass	Grasses	325	1
Woodland	Piñon, Juniper, Oak	3,319	14
Coniferous Forest	Pine, Fir	1,079	5
Cultivated		447	2
TOTAL		23,760	100

*Modified from U.S. National Resources Planning Board 1942:250.

This is due in large part to the great distances which pine pollen travels; therefore, the count does not clearly correspond with the vegetation on the collection site. Similar soil samples were taken for the Brantley Reservoir study in the Seven Rivers area from the surface of archaeological sites. The combined samples show similar nonrepresentation of the flora in the vicinity of the collections, and the flora seems to be a cross section of species in the various biotic regions in the Pecos Basin. Percentage composition of the major constituents in the Brantley Reservoir samples are shown in Table 2.

It is clear that modern pollen samples from the area would place it in the Piñon-Juniper belt if direct observation did not prove to the contrary. Some technique of weighting contamination should be developed to overcome this problem, such as that developed by Schoenwetter (1970). The difference between this sample from Brantley Reservoir and Bryant's sample from the southern end of the Guadalupe Mountains may suggest some regularities of pollen distribution in the area.

The Seven Rivers area samples are from a desert shrub community while the pollen counts should suggest desert shrub commu-

TABLE 2
Combined Pollen Counts
from Four Surface Soil Samples
in Brantley Reservoir
N=734

TYPES OF FLORA	PERCENTAGES
Juniper	25.0
Pine	17.8
Grasses	11.6
Douglas fir	11.2
Sage	10.9
Cheno-Ams	5.4
Composites	3.4
Oak	1.2
Other	13.4

nity only if contamination factors could be computed. However, the means of computing these factors are unknown. The fact remains that in the desert shrub community, well over half the flora represented in the pollen could be construed as representative of coniferous forest pollen. Bryant's sample from the southern end of the Guadalupe Mountains similarly represents higher altitude vegetation.

This demonstrates that pollen samples, unless depositional or contamination factors are built in, are likely to represent broad regional (or even superregional) flora. In terms of paleoclimatic reconstruction, this contamination may mean that pollen samples are even better measures of large scale climatic change than might be presumed. Considering these factors, pollen samples taken from soil on open archaeological sites are probably more informative for paleoclimatic reconstruction than for reconstructing a human consumption pattern. Having smaller amounts of cultural interference reduces the possibility that human activities are selecting certain species. More information could be gleaned if pollen samples were available both off of archaeological sites (in the form of columns for measuring climatic change) and on sites (in terms of measuring human selectivity). This examination fairly well demonstrates the need for more specific kinds of data in order to make a stronger climatic model for the Holocene in the Pecos Valley.

RECAPITULATION OF ENVIRONMENTAL/ARCHAEOLOGICAL EVIDENCE AND PROBLEMS

To summarize the climatic record:

1. The Antevs (1955) model may not record drought per se.

2. The fluctuations of Antevs's model correspond very closely in time to major fluctuations in arboreal and nonarboreal pollen from Wolf Creek Canyon Ranch on the Peñasco River.

3. These fluctuations probably should not be interpreted as "droughts." They might be interpreted as fluctuations in the amount of depression of biotic zones or changes that increase the importance of grasses but alter numbers of trees and shrubs only slightly. However when taken to extreme, these fluctuations result in a decrease in arboreal conditions reflecting severe denudation of the landscape.

4. Specific major fluctuations can be inves-

tigated in terms of cultural and technological changes which can be associated through the establishment of a more accurate time scale in the Middle Pecos. Specifically at this time, in the Middle Pecos, it seems that:

(a) the Paleo-Indian period ended with a long-term climatic fluctuation with reduction of the AP/NAP ratio;

(b) the area may have been lightly occupied during the early or middle Archaic (6500 to 4500 B.P.);

(c) equalization of the AP/NAP ratio during the middle Archaic with high AP count about 2500 B.P. may mark a generally more mesic environment through the late Archaic with the late AP count representing an even more dramatic fluctuation to high AP but no good evidence for the "Fairbank Drought" as such;

(d) the occupation of the Middle Pecos Valley during this period (about 2500 B.P.) seems to show an increase in population density which might be the population climax of the Archaic;

(e) the period from 2100 to 1300 B.P. was marked by a dramatic and relatively long-standing reduction in AP counts; this period may be associated with the disappearance of the Archaic lifestyle or perhaps simply with some rather important technological changes of which the introduction of ceramics is the most apparent in the Middle Pecos at this time;

(f) after 1300 B.P. the vegetation once again reflects more mesic conditions. To the north and west of the Middle Pecos some people were establishing semipermanent structures. In the Middle Pecos the most significant change is the construction or accretion of large mounds of burned rock which may show an elimination of dependence on deer as a food resource and a heavier dependence on plant food distribution. Intensity of environmental utilization may be increasing as a result of a greater population using these plant resources;

(g) an increase in grass pollen about 600 B.P. correlates with the "Great Drought" in the Navahonian biotic province. In the Chihuahuan province there only seems to be increased intensity of use of the burned rock mounds and plant foods with many ring middens in the fourteenth and fifteenth centuries. In the Kansan province there is evidence of heavy bison exploitation and changes in ceramics and habitation patterns;

(h) after circa 400 B.P. there is ethnohistoric evidence but no archaeological evidence of utilization of the lowland Pecos environment with no material remains visible in the Seven Rivers area until the Anglo historic period;

(i) until about 100 years ago the environment in the Seven Rivers area was dominated by expanding grassland conditions. Conditions in the last 100 years have changed the environment to a scrub desert with little moisture retention by soils and high erosion rates.

Finer control of environmental variables from the archaeological record is quite possible. More pollen collection is needed for control of modern pollen deposition variables which will provide control for prehistoric samples. Excavation of faunal assemblages is called for along with the necessary dating procedures. Until some of these studies can be more fully carried out, any tacit causal *correlation* rather than mere association, of the apparent climatic changes with cultural and technological changes would be misleading.

AN ETHNOHISTORIC MODEL
OF HUMAN SUBSISTENCE AND SETTLEMENT IN THE MIDDLE PECOS:
THE MESCALERO CASE

The assumptions and utility of ethnographic analogy are well explicated (Binford 1967; Nelson 1973; Thomas 1973; Human Systems Research 1973). The application of this method to the Seven Rivers area is facilitated by the presence of excellent records concerning Mescalero Apache subsistence and settlement patterns (Basehart 1960). In order to formulate the relationship between habitat, subsistence, and settlement for aboriginal populations in the Middle Pecos, a model based on information for the Mescalero Apache has been developed to serve as a baseline for comparison with archaeological manifestations.

HISTORICAL DOCUMENTATION OF SETTLEMENT IN THE SEVEN RIVERS AREA

There is some specific documentary evidence that the Seven Rivers area was utilized by the Mescalero Apache in the last 400 years. The fact that the Mescaleros ranged widely throughout the Pecos Basin and beyond makes it undoubtable that the Seven Rivers area was used by the Apache. The intensity of use or the density of activities carried out at the mouth of the Seven Rivers cannot be accurately measured from known historic documents. Basehart's (1960: 63-91) list of Mescalero place names does not give any unusual significance to the Seven Rivers area. However, Spanish and United States documents with specific references to Mescaleros in the Seven Rivers vicinity are available.

Schroeder (1973: 5,9,11) provides three accounts of Mescalero presence in the Seven Rivers area during Spanish Colonial days in New Mexico. During the 1700s there is some evidence that the Mescaleros may have been driven out of this very area during chronic hostilities with the Comanches. Accounts by Spaniards are available from the Coronado, Espejo, and De Sosa journeys in the Pecos drainage. These accounts have not been detailed because of the ambiguities encountered in cursorily interpreting ethnographic and topographic identifications.

During the early Anglo-American period, Captain R. S. Ewell attacked an encampment of Mescaleros near the mouth of the Peñasco River on the Pecos (Thomas 1959: 27). It is probable that this group of Mescaleros were engaged in hunting antelope, the important resource noted for the Apache in this area (Thomas 1959: 32). Again, further documentary research of archives and records may provide more detailed information on the intensity of Mescalero use of the Seven Rivers area. For immediate purposes, evidence is overwhelmingly in favor of the proposition that the Mescaleros used the Seven Rivers area at some period as a part of their exploitation of the Pecos River Basin.

POPULATION SIZE AND TERRITORIAL AREA OF THE MESCALEROS

In trying to arrive at an estimate of the intensity of ethnohistoric Mescalero use of the area, it is important to estimate the Mescalero population and the extent to which this population controlled the range. By evaluating these variables, an estimate of Mescalero population density and the limits of the Mescalero territory may be reached. This provides some impression of the density of activity that might be expected in the Seven Rivers area during the historic aboriginal period.

Mescalero territory was divided into two areas. The nuclear area of the Mescalero territory was in the Sacramento Mountains. However, the intensive use of this area was probably the result of Anglo efforts to contain the Mescaleros in the historic period (Basehart 1960: 90-91). The maximum documented range of the Mescaleros covered an area from Durango, Mexico on the south to Las Vegas, New Mexico on the north, from the Rio Grande River on the west, to the middle portions of the Llano Estacado in the vicinity of Lubbock, and to below the junction of the Pecos and Rio Grande on the southeast (Basehart 1960: Map 5; Opler and Opler 1950: 1-2).

Restricting our interest to either the nuclear settlement area or the maximum range causes certain conflicts. A good approximation of the total area dominated by the Mescaleros is the extent of the drainage of the Pecos River Basin. While this boundary does not cover the entire range under complete Mescalero control, it also includes some areas that were not completely controlled by the Mescaleros. Most conveniently, however, the area of the Pecos River drainage system can be accurately calculated at about 193,375 sq miles (U. S. National Resources Planning Board 1942: 250).

There are no reliable estimates of Mescalero population until well into the containment and reservation times (Basehart 1971: 37-38). Mooney (1928: 13) estimated a population of 700 for the Mescaleros in 1690. In 1894 a population of 5,000 Mescaleros was recorded (Coues 1895: 748). A better estimate can probably be obtained through the calculation of the number of Mescalero bands and their sizes. Basehart states concerning the Mescalero:

An informed guess as to band size. . .[is]

that numbers range from about 45 to 300 men, women and children. The majority of bands at this time (1850s) were intermediate in size with a population of about 90 to 100 persons (1971: 38).

The existence of 24 major Mescalero band leaders (between 1853 and 1861) is reported (Basehart 1960: 127). Because of changes in leadership and fluidity of bands, some of these leaders probably were in the same band. Also, knowledge of band leaders to the south is limited (Basehart 1960: 128). Calculating 24 bands and the estimates of maximum, minimum, and median band size provides population estimates (Table 3).

TABLE 3
Estimate of Mescalero Population
in 1850

Individuals per Band		Total Population
45	minimum	1,080
90	mean	2,160
100	median	2,400
300	maximum	7,200

For a base date of 1850 it appears a sound estimate of Mescalero population is about 4,000 individuals. This combined with the computed range yields a population density of about 1 person per 48 sq miles (125 sq km). For comparison, the population density in the Pecos Basin in 1940 was about 3.1 persons per 1 sq mile or 2.6 persons per 1 sq km (U. S. National Resources Planning Board 1942: 248).

Based on these calculations, one Mescalero band of 100 persons would have an available nonoverlapping exploitative area of approximately 4,800 sq miles. The archaeological survey of Brantley Reservoir would represent about 1/100 of the total area for one band. Although Mescalero bands were not localized, paths, movement networks, or areas of high resource yields could be expected to be used repeatedly. This amount of territory indicates that one Mescalero band might well exploit the total cross section of environmental diversity within the Pecos Basin. It is fairly certain that individual Mescalero bands did depend upon resources available in every major environmental zone. The extent of this dependence and the structure of the exploitative pattern is the subject of the following section.

MESCALERO SUBSISTENCE

Castetter and Opler (1936) have inventoried the major plant food resources of the Mescalero in considerable detail. Basehart (1960) has outlined the important plant and animal resources with respect to Mescalero social structure and scheduling in a manner rarely available in ethnographic literature. This information allows for a more fully documented Mescalero subsistence and settlement system.

Critical Food Resources
(Fig. 6)

Basehart (1960: 10-60) gathered information on food. Examination of this data suggests that Mescalero foods can be ranked in order of their importance in the diet. Whether this ranking is actually a function of the nutritional value of foods exploited (i.e., the first ranked food contributes more nutritionally to the average Mescalero diet than the second ranked food) or whether this ranking is a measure of what the Mescaleros preferred to eat is not clearly established.

Animal Foods (Wild)

Deer are ranked by the Mescalero informants as the most "important" food resource (Bashehart 1960:11) even though deer was not necessarily the largest single contributor to Mescalero food needs. Importance may rest on such factors as the sex of the informant, a culturally instilled preference for the taste of deer, or even certain ideological reasons for eating deer, e.g., there is a Mescalero taboo on eating deer brain (Basehart 1960: 14).

A test for deer importance within the diet would be to excavate many different kinds of Mescalero archaeological sites and, assuming that deer bone was preserved, calculate whether deer actually were more frequently used in terms of gross caloric value. If it is assumed that large numbers of deer are consumed, then importance of deer has a twofold meaning: (1) it is the largest caloric contributor and (2) deer will be exploited by a Mescalero over any other *available* resource.

The availability of deer, though, is dependent on avoiding the depletion of the deer population and/or on being able to capture deer without starving in the search process. For purposes here, deer are considered to be most "important" in both these senses. The limiting conditions for which deer would not have been sought are what makes a system model of Mescalero subsistence complex.

Basehart (1960: 15) states, "Antelope provided a significant contribution to Mescalero food supply, being exceeded in quantitative terms only by deer and bison." This statement provides support and confirmation for the rank ordering of animal food resources in terms of their caloric yield.

Plant Foods (Wild)

Plant foods probably had equivalent importance to all animal foods in terms of caloric intake:

> The gathering of wild plant foods played a critical role in Mescalero subsistence patterns...The quantitative contributions of the major food plants equaled or exceeded the food supply obtained from hunting. Collecting activities provided a margin of subsistence safety in an envi-

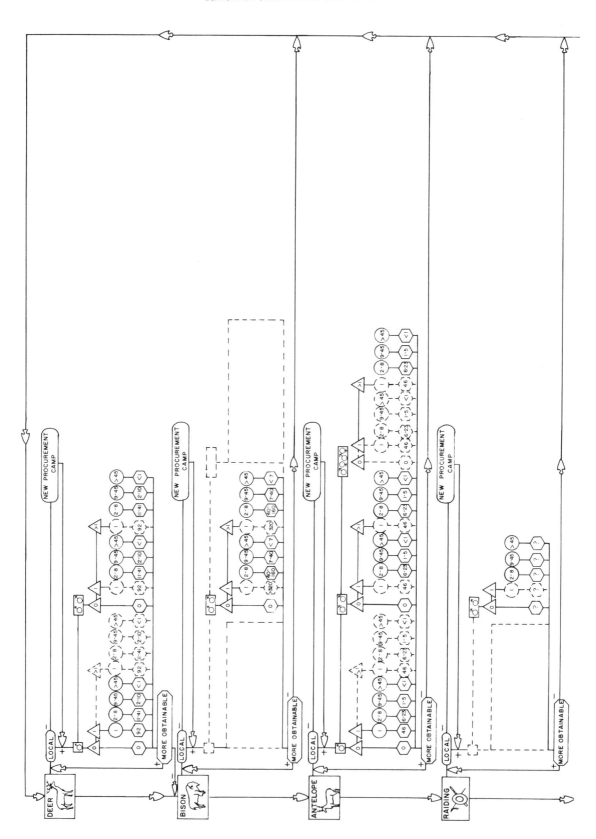

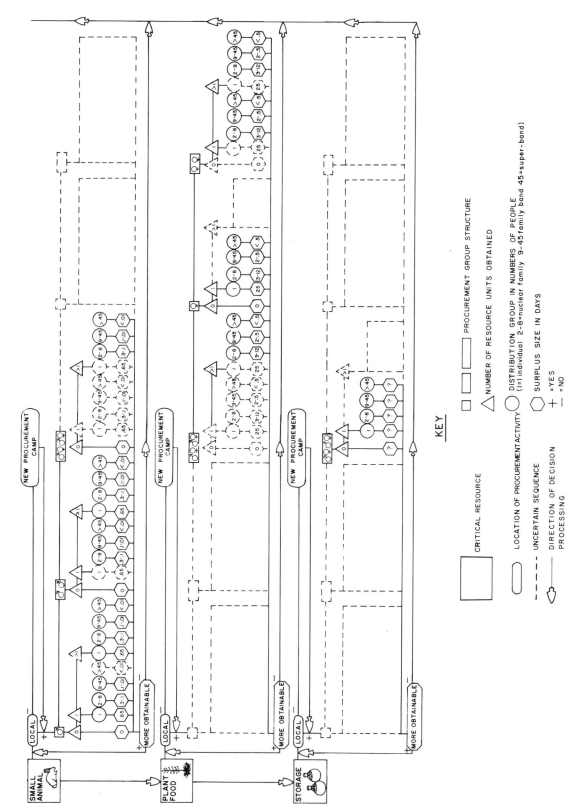

FIG. 6—Mescalero Subsistence Model.

ronment that was forbidding from many points of view. The emphasis on food gathering resulted in an important economic role for women, since they performed the major tasks of collecting.

The four wild crops of major importance were mescal, datil, piñon, and mesquite. The contribution of each of these crops to the family larder varied from year to year, except for mescal (Basehart 1960: 30).

It is difficult to tell which individual plant species were more important in caloric yield than individual animal species. As Basehart states, even the contribution of certain plants varied considerably. The problem of the value placed on plants in terms of their role in scheduling activities is even more difficult to interpret. The importance of plants may have varied considerably according to status and role conditions within the groups involved. For now, plant foods are lumped together instead of separated by species as to their importance. This procedure probably does not misrepresent the actual position of plants with respect to the decision making and the scheduling process. This is certainly a situation where quantitative data could help in interpretation. The position of plant foods succeeding all other animal foods in the model may have to be revised. However, the "social" value and the caloric value seem to be particularly contradictory as thorough reading of information on Mescalero social structure might indicate.

Raiding

Raiding is an indistinguishable part of a raiding and trading cycle in ethnohistoric times and has been ranked as the fourth most important contributor to subsistence. Place-

ment of raiding in this important position may also be an overinterpretation of the data.

It is difficult to estimate the contribution made by raiding to the Mescalero way of life with any degree of precision on the basis of ethnographic evidence (Basehart 1960: 94).

Again, the significance of social values encouraging this activity is difficult to measure in calories, unless one is willing to assume in this case that the caloric net returns of raiding (or any other activity) are also a direct measure of its social function and "importance."

After raiding, the hunting of small game has been ranked as a significant resource acquisition activity. "The Mescalero did not consider small animals particularly desirable, but such game was important as a subsistence supplement in time of scarcity" (Basehart 1960: 27). Prairie dogs and rabbits seem to have been particularly desirable small edible animals. This is another case where caloric importance of contribution to diet may not match the social value rankings given by the users.

Storage

Storage seems to be the last critical component of the resource system. In a strict sense storage does not increase the absolute volume of resources, but it does allow more flexibility in the scheduling of resource consumption. The storability and caching of foods can become a critical component of the resource system. Acquisition of reserve supplies can become a goal of hunting and gathering activities. There seems to be a particular relationship between storage and plant foods for the Mescaleros. Plants were collected above and beyond immediate use needs, and selection of plants was frequently with reference to their storage properties (Basehart 1960: 30, 35, 37).

Farming

Evidence of Mescalero farming is minimal and has not been included as a major resource activity (Basehart 1960: 58-59). Carter (1945) has suggested that dry farming in the Middle Pecos Basin would be rather unlikely due to a lack of moisture in the soil during the cool season. Evidence of other important activities with respect to resources might be suggested. However, the neatness with which the activities distinguished here can be tied to structuring of the resource acquisition, distribution, and availability patterns of the Mescaleros indicates that the model proposed has greatest utility in predicting subsistence activities at particular locations. The model is useful in predicting where the population will shift with respect to a rather complex set of conditions and decisions that must be made in order to perpetuate the cultural system. In terms of other factors to be discussed, critical resource acquisition can be tied to discrete but varying structures of acquisition, distribution, and utilization geared to specific foods within the system.

Location of Critical Resources

The ability to "depend" upon resources is a complex process of making the resources meet the needs of the group. If resources are not predictable in their abundance and distribution, then it is difficult to depend on them. It is my opinion that for the Mescaleros, resources were not dependable and predictable in measures of absolute confidence about their abundance at certain constant locations at a given time. But relative reliability of resources could be scaled with values ranging from no confidence to confidence in overabundance of resources at a given time and location. These predictions were based also on the capability of the given social structure to fully exploit the resources at a given time and location.

Basehart (1960: 30-31) points out that mescal ". . .is not subject to cyclic variations in quality and quantity". Datil, piñon, mesquite, and prickly pear were extremely variable in their abundance in a given location or the quality of fruit produced at a given time (Basehart 1960: 33-40). Simply knowing where particular food plant species grow and whether they produce seasonally is not likely to be a good basis on which to depend for a food supply. Yearly cycles may significantly reduce plant availability at given locations.

The argument can be more strongly stated for animal foods. This is not to claim that the Mescaleros did not have a better knowledge of their practical ecology than do modern anthropologists or that they were never in the right place to obtain food. However, it does mean that variable conditions required innovation of subsistence strategies which necessitated shifting distributions of population and different patterns of distribution and communication within segments of the population. If the location and intensity of use of certain locations as settlements, campsites, or other activities are to be predicted, it is necessary to predict how resources were used by the Mescaleros and how decisions were made to locate in order to exploit them.

Thomas (1972) has constructed a model for Great Basin aborigines that uses seasonality as the best predictive tool for settlement location. The Mescalero model does not depend on this factor as a *correlative* one although it may be *associated* with location of activity performance. The Mescalero subsistence system requires location of activities to be predicted on the basis of the location of *resources* as pointed out above, are not necessarily best predicted through seasonality (figs. 3 and 6).

If seasonality were the only issue, then informant response would show several conflicts in scheduling that would have very different locational parameters. For instance, the reported season for buffalo exploitation coincides closely with that of the piñon harvest. This would create a locational conflict which would have to be solved by a decision to exploit one of the resources or to place higher value on one alternative than another. Such a decision affects the social structure as well as the exploitive pattern. When an archaeological site is recorded in a certain location, it is not just representative of an optimum location for obtaining resources or a migratory response to season; it is a response also to social constants and the structure of the economic system.

Although we do not know precisely how the economic system operated for the Mescaleros in 1850, the high number of resources reported to have been exploited. during the fall suggests that storage of food resources may have been a crucial factor. Storage locations alone might indicate Mescalero settlement location better than any of the other predictors and probably as well as seasonal changes.

Social Pattern of Resource Acquisition

Not all resources were exploited by the Mescaleros using the same resource acquisition personnel. For each critical resource, the "typical" procurement structure(s) mentioned by Basehart (1960) have been delineated (fig. 6). This shows that different exploitation patterns existed within the structure of Mescalero society. The fact that these structures varied from resource to resource indicates that different values were probably attached to these resources. It confirms that preferred foods (animal foods) were procured by males or male dominated procurement groups. This structure should have value in predicting what kinds of activities and social structure might be associated with sites located for different resources or different spectra and abundance of resources. The division of labor is not simply tied to resource acquisition but is related complexly to it. By trying to understand the structure of this relationship, better predictive and descriptive models of archaeological remains can be formulated.

Social Pattern of Resource Distribution

The pattern of resource acquisition was no more dependent on the abundance and kind of resources available than it was on the social structures which claimed and processed these resources. A major variable in the social food chain seems to be the distribution group. The size of the distribution group has several discrete values, judging from the data that Basehart (1960) presented on Mescalero society.

Basehart (1971) also emphasizes the structure of Mescalero social divisions. He has termed the largest unit the band and has provided a range of size for bands. At the same time bands can divide along certain lines producing smaller bands or subbands (Basehart 1971: 40). In turn these subbands frequently were scattered over an area in nuclear family or extended nuclear family (with nonkin alliances) units. The variable kinship structure of these units appears to be similar to that reported for many Navajo "camps" by Henderson and Levy (1975). For the Mescaleros this point is emphasized, "Antelope hunting involved a minimum of formal organization. A man and his family might simply move out from a large encampment and head for antelope hunting grounds" (Basehart 1960: 16).

The existence of single individuals as procurement units is a logical possibility although no available references indicate that single individuals lived by themselves. Details of raiding and ritual are too incompletely known to eliminate the possibility that this is an important structural pattern.

Catch Size, Consumption, and Surplus

The ability to obtain resources is limited by certain biological and mechanical parameters as well as defined by availability of the resources. For example in piñon nut collection.

the maximum possible investment of energy in ideal conditions would yield 100 lbs of harvest per collector per day (Basehart 1960: 36). Similar limitations would be imposed with any resource. However, the size and structure of the procurement group could well improve quantity of catch size with some resources (i.e., buffalo). The size of the catch would interrelate with the availability of the resource, the size of the procurement group, and the size of the supporting distribution group. When catch size does not perfectly balance with these variables, on one side there is surplus. On the other there is a readjustment the location or the structure of the acquisition group or of the structure of the distribution group.

In the case of surplus, it is assumed that surplus was preserved and stored although it is conceivable that it was gorged down and/or wasted. However, little information concerning how or where foods were stored is available. The system outlined could not be adjusted easily for extensive storage facilities if the supply were unpredictable in a certain location. Mescal "was one of the most prized foods in the Mescalero subsistence inventory, both because it is not subject to cyclic variations in quality and quantity and because of its excellent storage properties" (Basehart 1960: 30-31). Gifford (1940: 16) lists several alternative methods for Mescalero food storage including cave storage and tree storage in skin bags and pottery containers. Long term storage might decrease in importance in a society with increasing mobility (horses) and predatory (raiding) activities such as the Mescaleros were undertaking when many of the observations used in this analysis were made.

In the formal model (fig. 6) under each of the specified conditions of catch size, a surplus value has been estimated. The figures are rough estimations of surplus expressed in number of days of surplus under each condition; these figures are based on known caloric values of foodstuff (Watt and Merrill 1963) or on very roughly estimated values. Detailed patterns of plant and animal consumption are unknown. Ethnographically, the parts of plants and animals used and the processing techniques are rarely known. Reconstruction of these patterns may be possible from archaeological remains.

DIFFICULTIES WITH THE ETHNOGRAPHIC MODEL

A normative model based on the subsystems recognized in the Mescalero subsistence-settlement model can be roughly sketched for the major archaeological horizons visualized in the Seven Rivers area. Six variables are of particular interest: critical food resources, settlement structure/resource locations, resource procurement group structure, normal size of catch of resource, the group to which resources are normally redistributed, and the storability of foods in the cultural system. It is the goal of future archaeological work in the area to define more precisely and operationalize archaeological tests for the identification of these subsystems and their social correlates.

The Mescalero model may not apply to a hunting-gathering economy in the Brantley Reservoir area at all time periods since different resource exploitation systems probably operated depending on cultural and ecological conditions. The synchronic Mescalero model (fig. 6) and the less complete diachronic model (Table 4) follow closely the "production, consumption, and transfer" components fundamental in modern concepts of economic anthropology (LeClaire 1962). On the basis of excavated faunal and floral materials, analysis of settlement patterns, and intrasite patterning, inferences can be made regarding critical food resources, resource related settlement patterns or scheduling, and perhaps the size and composition of procurement groups and redistribution groups. At this point these subsystems can only be reconstructed by analogy.

DISCUSSION OF THE DIACHRONIC MODEL

(Table 4)

It is assumed that the Paleo-Indian economy was largely a big game hunting one. However, the real nature of the balance between plant and animal resources and time spent in procuring them is unknown. It is improbable that the limited Paleo-Indian materials recovered in the Seven Rivers area will allow much to be said about the Paleo-Indian occupation.

The Archaic presents a much more interesting problem. Evidence from Fresnal Shelter indicates that the Archaic occupants of the Middle Pecos may have subsisted heavily on deer as did the Mescaleros. However, the degree of similarity of home territory of the Archaic peoples with Mescaleros is completely unknown. If bison had a distribution similar to the ethnohistoric case, then the Archaic home territory may have been about equal to that of a Mescalero band in order to utilize bison. This would in turn require more time spent on the Llano Estacado because of the limitations of foot transport in Archaic times. This would conceivably affect the whole remainder of the procurement, catch, and redistribution system presented.

The Ceramic occupants of the Middle Pecos also seem to have had a critical resource base different from other time periods. The analogy of burned rock mounds and ring middens to large mescal baking pits has been stressed by Mera (1943), Greer (1965), and Shutler and Shutler (1962). The endemic use of large numbers of burned rock in this manner does not appear to begin until the Ceramic occupation although equal amounts of burned

TABLE 4
A Diachronic Cross Classification of Different Factors
in the Economic Systems of Human Population in the Middle Pecos Area

FACTOR	PALEO	ARCHAIC	CERAMIC	APACHE	FRONTIER ANGLO-AMERICAN
Critical Resources	Bison Herbivores Plants	Deer Small animals Plants	Small animals Plants	Herbivores Raiding Plants	Food Production
Settlement Structure	Free wandering	Restricted wandering	Limited range restricted wandering	Central-based	Simple nuclear
Procurement group structure for first resource	Multi-male	Single male or small units	Community or cooperative band	Multi-male	Single male
Redistribution	Family/band	Family	Band	Family/band	Super community
Storage capability	Days	Weeks	Months	Weeks	Months/years

rock in dispersed camp scatters may occur in the Archaic. This fact may reflect an increased dependence or modified exploitation system for the succulent plants in the Middle Pecos during the Ceramic period. There is no way at present of gauging the prevalence or nature of the use of these burned rock aggregations other than by reference to ethnohistoric examples. Replicative experiments should be considered (Ashbee and Cornwall 1961) as a feasible approach to this problem. Although the utilization of such burned rock aggregates may have been the same by the Mescaleros and other aboriginal and earlier groups in the area, the evidence is not conclusive. Whether the Mescaleros actually used ring middens or simply the mescal pit is uncertain (Greer 1965). If the Ceramic occupants had modified their technology for exploiting plant foods, this may be a reflection of changes throughout the cultural system.

Emphasis on plant food exploitation would require several modifications with respect to the group structure involved in harvesting and processing these plants.

In this brief discussion I have not intended to show explicitly that the variables mentioned in the model (Table 4) change in the way shown. I have attempted only to show that (1) there is some evidence of change in the economic systems through time in the Middle Pecos and (2) this change may not reflect only the composition of intake of food resources but also affects and was effected by changes in many other components of the cultural system. Demonstrating the existence of changes such as these and outlining in detail the relations of food resources and settlement patterns to social structures (as has been done for the Mescalero case) are goals of future archaeological work in the Seven Rivers area and the Middle Pecos.

ARCHAEOLOGICAL SURVEY AND THE PREHISTORIC SETTLEMENT SYSTEMS OF THE SEVEN RIVERS AREA

THE NATURE OF THE SURVEY

The archaeological survey centered at the mouth of the Seven Rivers and the nearby sections of the Pecos River. The choice of this area is not the result of a deductive attempt to randomly sample the Pecos environment or to build prehistoric subsistence and settlement systems from archaeological materials. Rather, the area was defined for us by the U.S. Bureau of Reclamation. This area is not simply a target area for archaeological and theoretical anthropological tests of hypotheses; it is also an area scheduled for extensive land modification and eventual flooding by the proposed Brantley Reservoir. This reservoir will flood the area of the confluence of the Seven Rivers and the Pecos River. It will also directly affect about 30,000 acres (121.4 sq km) of land and flood, bury, destroy, or modify in some manner 92 historic and prehistoric archaeological sites.

The archaeological survey indicates inhabitants were in the area to be flooded as long ago as 10,000 B.P. and that periodic but recurrent occupation and use of the area has continued to the present. Further archaeological work through excavation of materials in the Seven Rivers area is planned. The assessment of the value of the previously outlined research orientation can be evaluated best by its utility in guiding an excavation program.

SURVEY MECHANICS AND RELIABILITY OF COVERAGE

In the Seven Rivers area locating sites was dictated by the nature of the ground cover. It is estimated that about half of the total survey area was under impenetrable salt cedar swamps (fig. 2) formed in the recent alluvial delta behind Lake McMillan. Although during the survey the salt cedar area was almost completely dry, the probability of locating sites was unlikely. Several feet of silt have accumulated in this area in the last 75 years burying any archaeological material which may be there. The remainder of the reservoir area was relatively easy to cover by foot; about 15 to 25% was under cultivation, primarily in alfalfa. Although much of this area was intensively covered, no sites were located in irrigated fields. This may be due to the large-scale land modification necessary to maintain field levels suitable for irrigation.

The remaining 25% of the total 30,000 acres to be flooded (about 7,500 acres) was covered intensively on foot. Strips of salt cedar and areas adjoining sites that were covered by growth also were examined closely. The maximum distance between the two most distant sites located in the area to be affected by the reservoir was about 20 miles. Most sites were located in a much smaller area between McMillan Dam and the proposed location of Brantley Dam (fig. 2).

The survey was accomplished with a crew of nine. One crew member was employed full-time contacting landowners to obtain permission to cross land so the rest of the crew could look for archaeological materials. This method led to close contact with the local residents which resulted in the collection of detailed information on local inhabitants' personal knowledge of archaeology and history. This information was used to aid in a better understanding of the present community and the distribution of archaeological materials.

The remaining crew of eight was divided into two survey teams. Two teams allowed more effective utilization of the survey

41

vehicle and time. Coverage of the ground was fairly intensive. Crew members were generally spaced 25 to 75 m apart. The survey forms utilized were designed to be explicit for this survey and to ask largely "objective" questions. Most of the forms were filled out by the two crew chiefs fostering less variability in responses. Every site location was marked on U.S.G.S. 7.5 minute topographic maps. The initial survey form was completed as rapidly as possible. Photographs were taken, and no surface collection was made. Instead of collecting surface materials, the crew would carefully look at surface artifacts and report the presence of tools, ceramics, and other kinds of artifacts.

Bousman (1974*a*) had already located 22 sites in a week-long reconnaissance of the area providing some idea of site variability. Our initial survey was a complete inventory, and a rough attempt was made to stratify the sites by features of their assemblage or environment. This stratification was revised after the field season was completed and is reported below. During our inventory phase, 70 sites were located in about three weeks. This brought the total number of recorded sites to 92.

After having roughly stratified the sites into small and large, burned rock present and burned rock absent categories (a fourfold matrix), grab-sample collections were made at the smallest sites, test holes with a posthole digger were sunk to check on the depth of deposit, and pollen samples were collected if appropriate. Smaller sites were chosen for collection due to time limitations, for comparability between sites, and to provide a comparison with larger sites in subsequent field work. Each site collected was marked with a 2 ft piece of reinforcing bar driven into the ground for future reidentification. A few sites turned out to be larger, denser, and more complex than estimated by the locational inventory survey. A total of 22 archaeological sites were surface collected. These in the end

provided a cross section of all site types. During this process, site outlines were mapped by the use of a pocket transit and the triangulation method. In this way the area of the distribution of surface material was more adequately portrayed than by pacing or tape measurements. Placing postholes demonstrated that these sites were largely confined to the top 20 cm of soil.

One controlled surface collection was conducted at Site X29ED56 (the Dolomite Dunes Site). This site, measuring approximately 200,000 sq m, was gridded into 10 x 10 m units. Approximately 1,800 sq m (1%) of this site were collected in 2 x 2 m units.

SURVEY ANALYSIS

Spaulding (1960) in a now classic statement of the scope of archaeology, divided data into three general dimensions and an interrelationship matrix between these dimensions. Some basis will be provided on which these dimensions of time, space, and style can be interrelated for the cultural sequence in the Seven Rivers survey area. The spatial and stylistic associations will be discussed later. A chronometric system has been developed for the Seven Rivers survey material. Some chronological scaling is essential for an understanding of culture change, but it is essential to understand that the procedures used herein for chronological scaling are still in need of refinement and testing.

Temporal Placement

There are two "time markers" that were used in assigning temporal position to prehistoric archaeological materials. These two diagnostics were ceramics and projectile points; more reliable chronometric indices will be necessary in future work. The nature of this survey did not allow the collection of *in situ* materials for radiocarbon dating or the gathering of any other chronometric information. The general surface nature of many sites in the reservoir may make the collection of reliable chronometric samples very difficult in the final analysis.

Ceramics

Mera (1943) established the type system and affiliations of most of the ceramic styles found in the region of southeastern New Mexico. The survey of Brantley Reservoir located 35 sites with prehistoric ceramics. This may not represent the entire number of sites that have or have had ceramics on them because surface collection is a favorite pasttime of many residents in the area. Very few sherds were counted on any sites; estimates of total number of sherds exposed on the surface of any site is less than 100 although subsurface conditions may vary somewhat.

Types recorded in the survey were recently described by Runyan and Hedrick (1973). The major types were Chupadero B/W, El Paso Brown, Jornada Brown, and Three Rivers R/T (fig. 7). A few sherds of Lincoln B/R were also tentatively identified, but these were not collected. Only in a few cases are types in association with radiocarbon dated sites in the Pecos Valley (Jelinek 1967; Greer 1968a, 1968b). Outside the Pecos Valley these types are known from tree ring dated contexts (Breternitz 1966). However, there are very few dates to accurately demonstrate the span of the dated types or variation in dates in subtypes or subregions. Clearly the dated context of these types is not closely controlled, nor can various hypothesized varieties be tied to more limited temporal or spatial spans at this time as has been done for other ceramic sequences in the Southwest.

The types recognized from the Brantley Reservoir survey do not represent the entire spectrum of sherd types found in the Pecos Valley (Honea 1973; Jelinek 1967; Runyan and Hedrick 1973; Mera 1943; Kelley 1966). When larger sherd samples are gathered in the Seven Rivers area from controlled contexts, more careful study of the ceramics will be warranted. Particularly, dated contexts are needed on the Pecos River itself. The presence of Three Rivers R/T at some sites in the Brantley Reservoir may indicate a later occupation on a portion of the sites where ceramics are found. Control of ceramic dates is not available for the Seven Rivers study area and must await future study.

Projectile Points

The use of projectile points and ceramics as time markers leads to many problems in the interpretation of these items from the archaeological record. Projectile points are particularly controversial when used in seriation schemes. Projectile points located during the survey have been seriated on one attribute, neck width. Jelinek (1967: 91) suggests that the "midstem diameter" (neck width) and the "base midstem diameter" may show general "chronological trends" when metrically ordered. He suggests that Archaic and later projectile points may be distinguished on this attribute. Corliss (1972) has demonstrated for the northern Great Basin and northwest Cordilleran that greater neck widths tend to be associated with early spear throwing complexes and that a diminuation of neck width represents a transformation to a more recent bow and arrow technology. Neck width seems to be a valuable trait with which to order projectile points chronologically.

The 53 projectile points from the collections and from on-site silhouette tracings were measured for neck width. Most of these specimens were fragments, but fragments usually were represented by bases. The results of this ordered sequence are presented in Fig. 8 and 9. The conformity of projectile points on either tail of the distribution to suspected chronological position lends some support to this ordering technique. Paleo-Indian points occurred at the large end of the distribution

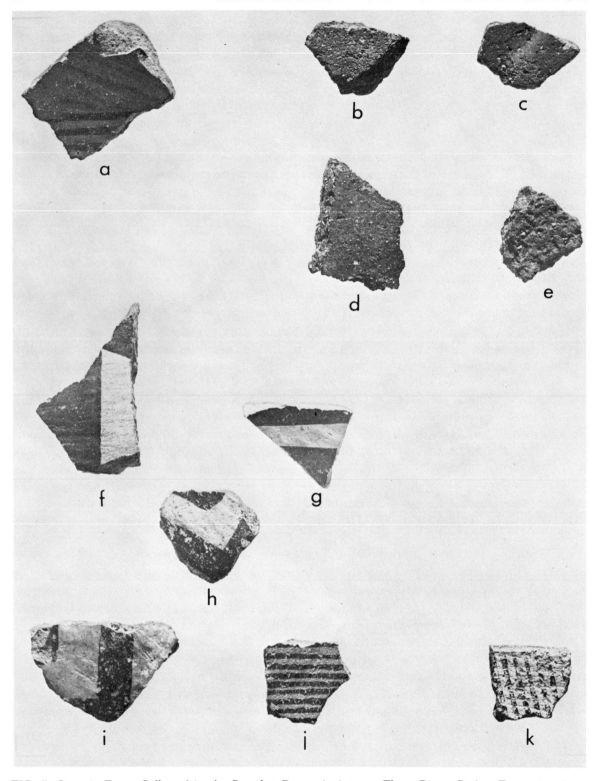

FIG. 7–Ceramic Types Collected in the Brantley Reservoir Area–*a*, Three Rivers Red-on-Terracotta; *b*, *c*, Jornada Brownware; *d*, *e*, El Paso Brownware; *f–k*, Chupadero Black-on-White. Sherds are approximately life-size.

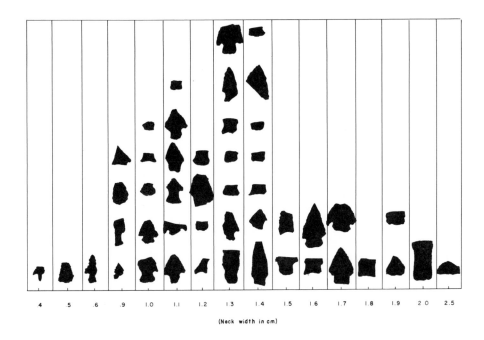

FIG. 8–Chart Showing Silhouettes of Projectile Points Scaled According to Neck Width. (Artifacts ¼ natural size).

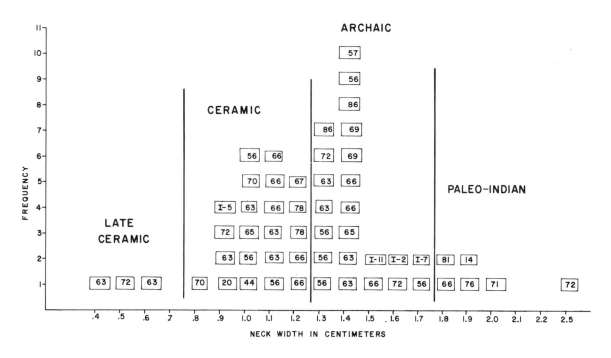

FIG. 9–Distribution of Neck Widths of Projectile Points from Sites and Isolated Finds Recorded during Site Survey and Site Collections of Brantley Reservoir. (An *I* precedes isolated finds. All other numbers in boxes are preceded by X29ED indicating site number. Several artifacts recorded in this figure are not included in Fig. 8).

(Folsom, Plainview, Jay) while commonly accepted late types (Scallorn and Perdiz) were at the opposite extreme. The projectile point neck width distribution also provides a hypothetical Archaic/Ceramic separation. While the reality of any of these divisions must be suspect, the method does allow the provisional placement of certain sites into a time dimension. In the absence of better dating procedures, this is a useful methodology.

Ceramic and projectile point "time markers" allow placement of 40 prehistoric sites from the Brantley Reservoir survey into broad archaeological horizons. From this a provisional index of occupational intensity of the Middle Pecos Valley can be outlined: Paleo-Indian components (6), Archaic components (9), Ceramic components (35), sites with unknown components (36), sites with at least one known component (40). This kind of ordering of site component information suggests that some kind of inference about the actual population levels in different prehistoric periods may be possible. Of course several assumptions are necessary to make population estimates. Some of these possibly untenable assumptions are: (1) projectile points have a relatively constant relationship to population; (2) the resources and utilization of the Brantley area environment are equally important to all the prehistoric economies of the Middle Pecos; and (3) modern artifact hunters have not selectively collected certain projectile point types. However, if we realize that currently there are tremendous limitations on population estimates of this nature, some interesting results are still obtained. Estimating that the Paleo-Indian period is about 4,000 years in duration, the Archaic 5,000 years in duration, and the Ceramic period only about 600 years, a rather remarkable transformation occurs during Ceramic times. The number of sites of Paleo-Indian and Archaic affiliations are approximately the same when the length of the respective periods is taken into account. How-

ever the Ceramic period shows a growth of several orders of magnitude in occupational intensity (population). Clearly this observation at present is not well controlled, but it does provide a model of change which needs to be explained with more complete control over variables which tend to distort the usefulness of component counts for population estimates. This kind of information can be obtained through a complete excavation program.

Locational Data

In order to summarize locational data for each of these archaeological horizons, a nearest neighbor statistic was calculated for each classificatory period (Table 5) using the statistic provided by Whallon (1973). All prehistoric sites in the survey area (approximately 122 sq km) were found to be on an average of 0.6 km from the nearest other prehistoric site in the survey area. The nearest neighbor statistic (R) for these sites showed a slight tendency towards clustering (R = .75) where R = 1.00 is approximately random spacing. This is probably a reflection of the concentration of sites in the area south of McMillan Dam in the confluence of the Seven Rivers. The statistics for the remainder of the sites classified by horizon are presented in Table 5.

These data must be interpreted carefully. Generally the sample sizes for sites of known temporal affiliations are too small, and the greatest linear relationship seems to be with the number of sites in each sample. If we accept that an R of 1.00 is approximately random distribution of sites over the geographic surface, R approaching zero (0) is a tightly clustered distribution, and R approaching 2.15 is maximally spaced on the geographic surface (Whallon 1973; Hagget 1966: 232-33), then only one statistic is of great interest. The close approximation of maximum spacing of identifiable Paleo-Indian

TABLE 5

Nearest Neighbor Statistics for Prehistoric Sites
of Known and Unknown Temporal Placement

Temporal Periods	(N)	Average distance to nearest neighbor (km)	R (nearest neighbor statistic)
All prehistoric	77	.6	.75
All ceramic	35	.8	.84
Ceramic on basis of points	10	1.8	1.01
Archaic	9	2.2	1.17
Paleo-Indian	6	4.8	2.14

sites in the survey area is descriptively valid. This may reflect the tendency of these sites to be strung along the length of the river (north to south) while in other horizons occupation is more randomly spaced or clustered at the confluence of the Pecos River and Seven Rivers.

In contrast, spacing approaches clustering on the Lakewood Terrace south of McMillan Dam for the Ceramic horizon. This suggests some changes in the exploitative economy of the horizons. However, this occurrence could also be due to geological transformations (such as buried sites of early periods in the valley itself) or recent land modification (field clearing or silting behind Lake McMillan). Although there are not sufficient data to test these alternatives now, more data can be gathered on the economic changes in critical resources, and this seems the most fruitful approach in future excavation and site collection strategies.

Functional Data

During the survey, a consistent effort was made to place archaeological sites into an explicitly descriptive framework on the basis of gross differences between sites. The existence of differences between site manifestations in the Middle Pecos Valley on the basis of morphological details has been of interest to archaeologists in the area for some

time. Recent work in the Middle Pecos Region has recognized several kinds of sites in the area (Jelinek 1967; Katz and Katz 1974; Shafer 1970); however, in these cases little information has been available to explain the differences recognized. The classification here is an attempt to place descriptive classification on an explanatory level.

The classification can best be visualized as a decision tree. Although this is an extremely simple key, as far as the archaeology of the Middle Pecos is concerned, these types of sites can be readily recognized but perhaps under different names by different workers (fig. 10). Some of the structural variability in artifact and burned rock scatters of the large sort is visible in the plates (figs. 11, 12, 13, 14).

It has been most difficult without more precise maps of site areas to distinguish between "large" and "small" sites. It seems probable that upon complete mapping of sites, an actual bimodal distribution of site size will emerge. These differences in site size also suggest several important differences in function between these sites. Explicitly identifying these functions and relating them to morphology should be a goal of further research.

These problems are illustrated by the lack of independence of site size on the presence of burned rock suggested in the cross-classification table (Table 6). For now artifact and burned rock scatters (large) are defined as sites with an estimated surface area exceeding 3,000 sq m or with a probable buried surface exceeding that figure (as at some of the mound sites), burned rock present, and relatively higher densities of chipped stone debris. Artifact and burned rock scatters (small) have areas less than 17,000 sq m, burned rock, and at the larger sizes very low chipped stone debris densities. Artifact scatters (large) have surface areas upwards of 14,000 sq m but without burned rock. Artifact scatters (small) have surface areas less than 19,000 sq m and no burned rock. The reason for overlap in some of these attributes between sites types is due to the entrance of some subjective evaluation of survey information and the fact that the sites are probably continuously distributed on some of these attributes. Such things as suspected buried materials, recording of several distinct activity areas at one site, and the roughness of survey estimates help explain the overlapping variability at the extremes of each of the site type

categories. The average characteristics of each type are still suggestive of the real variation between sites.

TABLE 6
Cross Classification of Prehistoric Site Types

	Artifact/Burned Rock Scatter	Artifact Scatter	Total
Small	24	29	53
Large	21	3	24
Total	45	32	77

Judge (1974) has shown that different activities are represented on different kinds of sites during the Paleo-Indian period in the Middle Rio Grande Valley. This suggests that the cross-classification presented above may be used to distinguish activities. Future work can operationally define the two variables of site size and amount of burned rock more precisely and should suggest other variables that

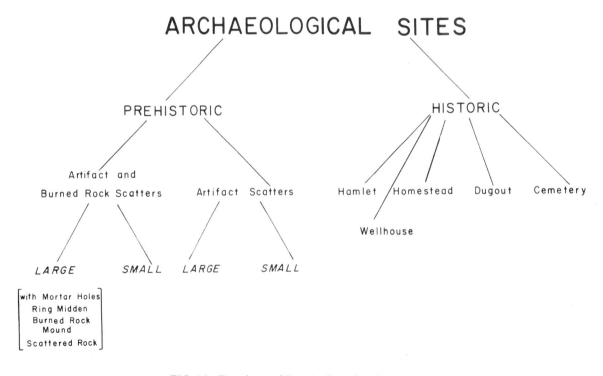

FIG. 10—Typology of Sites in Brantley Reservoir.

FIG. 11—Example of a Mortarhole Site (X29ED87).

FIG. 12—Example of a Burned Rock Mound (X29ED4).

FIG. 13—Example of a Ring Midden (X29ED6).

FIG. 14—Example of a Burned Rock Scatter (X29ED3).

make these types of sites more discretely different. Gathering this information on a continuous variable scale might more readily show a linear relationship of site size and burned rock.

It is further suggested that a good indication of functional difference can be found not only in nominal (present/absent) phenomena but also in frequencies of artifacts and ecofacts in the archaeological assemblage. The direct analogy between resource procurement areas and settlement locations must await further investigation. Similarly, no controlled samples of excavated faunal or floral data have yet been made which specifically can be tied to archaeological locations. This restricts the ability to distinguish functional differences between sites on the basis of archaeological ecofacts. The most consistent information on which to establish functional variability at this time between sites in the Brantley Reservoir is artifact assemblages.

Percent frequency graphs were constructed from the number of sites of each type for which the presence of certain artifact categories was recorded (fig. 15). Tables 7 (p. 59), 8a (p. 62), and 8b (p. 65) provide the data from which these graphs were constructed. The distribution of these artifacts for each site type in the Brantley Reservoir sample forms the best expected frequencies for artifact categories for the Middle Pecos area as a whole. We now have a model of the artifact assemblage on the different kinds of sites for the Middle Pecos. These data are not completely consistent or in sufficient quantities to warrant sophisticated statistical testing of specific hypotheses at this time. It does appear that some of the deviations about the average values for all the sites in the Brantley Reservoir inventory may be significant in indicating the variations in function for the previously defined site types. From these deviations explanations will be hypothesized for the differences, and functional models of activities for the different site types will be developed.

Functional Model:
Artifact and Burned Rock Scatters (Large)

Taking the artifact classes that are usually considered to be representative of chipped stone tool manufacture (cores, bifaces, hammerstones), the distribution of these classes on artifact and burned rock scatter (large) sites would indicate that this activity was only of average importance on these sites. Chipped stone tools are poorly represented compared to the ground stone complex (manos and metates). The large numbers of burned rock on these sites and the ground stone tools conform to what might be decided intuitively about these sites: they appear to be high intensity camping stations. The moderate representation of chipped stone tools and the large representation of grinding tools and ceramics further suggests that other types of sites might show inverse proportions of these artifact types. The fact that this *does occur* leads us to suspect that different frequencies of tools and artifacts are significantly associated with different types of sites as defined here. Some functional validity is thereby confirmed for this site typology system.

Functional Model:
Artifact and Burned Rock Scatters (Small)

Small sites with burned rock on the surface seem to conform, in general, to the large sites with burned rock in the composition of the tool assemblage; the high number of retouched pieces seems to be the most marked deviation. Retouched pieces are taken to be evidence of animal hide processing tools. The difference between artifact and burned rock scatters (large) and artifact and burned rock scatters (small) sites is not *just* in gross amounts of human activity. If the site inventory observations conform in any way to the true representation of assemblage differences, small sites may represent sites used more extensively for animal processing activities than were the large sites which conform more to a plant processing site pattern. This is why points and retouched pieces are more common in small scatters of artifacts and burned rock than in the larger sites where manos and metates have high proportions compared to the smaller sites (fig. 15).

These tool assemblage and site morphology differences seem to represent a marked variation in the site use patterns, perhaps focusing on different social structural variables related to resource variation. It is suggested that arti-

fact and burned rock scatter (large) sites were located with respect to plant food resources and inhabited by larger social units. Males were traveling to other locations for chipping activities and also away from these large aggregations for hunting activities and the hunting associated activity of preliminary animal food processing. On the other hand, artifact and burned rock scatter (small) sites were located more with respect to animal food resources. Men did not have to travel so far for resources from these smaller camps as they

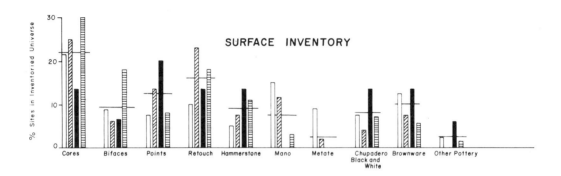

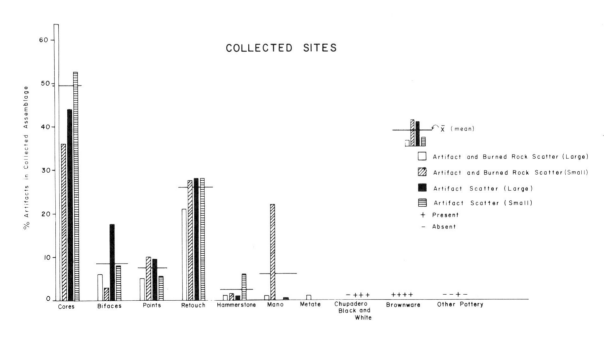

FIG. 15—Frequency of Sites from Inventory Survey with Artifact Type Present (*upper*) and Frequency of Artifact Types on Sites Collected (*lower*).

would from larger camps. Processing of animal foods was done more intensively on these smaller sites because it was easier to transport animals from close by kill locations. Small family groups were occupying these sites, and women were spending less time in gathering plant foods and processing them and more time in processing hides and animal food.

Functional Model: Artifact Scatters (Large)

These sites, identified by large scatters of chipped stone, ceramics, and the absence of burned rock, are the most tenuous of the site types. Only three of these sites were identified in the Brantley Reservoir area. The nearest neighbor statistic (R = .26) indicates that they are highly clustered within the survey area. These sites may represent a highly specialized and necessarily localized activity in the entire Brantley Reservoir area.

The tool assemblage on these three sites lacked ground stone tools. However, ceramics were more abundant than in any other type of site. Low representation of cores and bifaces was also noticeable. Projectile points were present in every case.

It is suggested that these sites are activity areas associated with hunting activities. Their concentration on the bluffs of the Gypsum Land soil association indicates that this area might have been a particularly advantageous one for observing movements of large animals over a great area. These sites also might have held some special attraction so that these mammals would congregate in the area. Perhaps salt was available here or a major game trail passed through this area. Tools seem to reflect both a staging area for hunting activities and the processing of animal foods. Below average amounts of chipped stone core reduction were also observed. No particularly desirable raw material sources for chipped stone tools were located in this section of the Gypsum Land. The presence of pottery in every case might appear to be anomalous. If

this were a major game trail, it might also have been a major thoroughfare for people. The pottery may represent storage of water or of certain animal by-products in either the staging or processing part of activities on these sites.

Functional Model: Artifact Scatters (Small)

These sites are similar in assemblage to the large artifact scatter sites. Ground stone tools are rare. However, these small sites outstrip other types in the presence of cores and bifaces which occur in greater proportions than on other types of sites. The presence of hammerstones, retouched pieces, and projectile points are not inconsistent with visualizing these sites as areas for manufacture of chipped stone tools or selection of raw materials. However, in many cases the presence of suitable on-site raw materials for chipping is very doubtful. Ground stone tools were distinctive in their manufacture from a sandstone material. Sandstone, though, was not seen to outcrop naturally anywhere in the Seven Rivers vicinity. The presence of manos and ceramics on these sites stresses the great weakness of the method used here in consistently sorting out site types. It must be remembered that the data are insufficient to unerringly place every site in either one morphological category or another, and functional categories must be held in even greater suspicion. Particularly with artifact scatter (small) sites, we may be simplifying the case by making one morphological category correspond to one functional category. Some of these sites may be chipping areas, and others may be more similar in function to the artifact scatter (large) sites but simply smaller in area and intensity of use. The fact that this system has lumped temporal categories set up earlier must also be remembered. Another drawback of the system used here is the implication that sites functioned in identical ways for 10,000 years; this was probably not the case. The difference in the material remains in activities from one horizon to another was probably not a quantum change in organization but largely a gradual change in frequency of activities and in population density. Only controlled surface collections and excavation can give finer control over these variables, and confirm, modify, or destroy the model set out for the functions of these sites.

Locational Analysis and Site Typology

Nearest neighbor measurements were performed on the site type system (Table 9) as well as on the chronological system (Table 5). The site types consistently showed random patterning except for the artifact scatter (large) sites as noted above. It is possible to do much more with spatial and locational analysis than has been done to date. Resource analysis for floral, faunal, and lithic sources could be correlated with site locations. Also calculating 1st, 2nd, 3rd and higher order nearest neighbors might show that there was a sharp or distinguishable break in clusters of sites at some value of discrete nearest neighbor combinations. From the functional models presented for the site typology established above we hypothesize that: (1) artifact and burned rock scatter (large) sites would be more distant from artifact and burned rock scatter (small) sites than they would be from other artifact and burned rock scatter (large) sites; (2) artifact and burned rock scatter (large) sites would be more distant from artifact scatter (small) sites than from any other site; (3) artifact and burned rock scatter (small) sites and artifact scatter (small) sites would show little relationship to each other in distance. A preliminary test of this kind of inference was made (Table 10, p. 66).

These tests show that the intuitively derived spatial site types may need modification. Artifact and burned rock scatter (large) sites are as close to other sites of this type as they are to artifact and burned rock scatter

(small) sites—this may show that artifact and burned rock scatter (small) sites are maximally distant from other settlement areas or independent of the spacing of the other site types. Artifact and burned rock scatter (large) sites are closer to artifact scatter (small) sites than to other artifact and burned rock scatter (large) sites—this may demonstrate that artifact scatter (small) sites do indeed represent some sort of resource area with which artifact and burned rock scatter (small) sites are located. The greater spacing of artifact and burned rock scatter (small) sites from artifact scatter (small) sites may indeed confirm the satellite status of artifact scatter (small) sites to artifact and burned rock scatter (large) sites—this may indeed support the independence of artifact and burned rock scatter (small) and artifact scatter (small) sites in their functional characteristics.

It seems clear that more spatial and locational analysis based on a tighter perspective of site similarities and differences in assemblages may begin to have predictive value in locating sites in the Middle Pecos as well as providing a measure of association between certain types of sites and their assemblages.

COLLECTION ANALYSIS

After the initial locational survey was completed, 22 sites were selected for total surface collection. All sites collected were those sites that were indicated in the inventory survey to consist of only a few pieces of lithic debris. The sites were collected, mapped to establish actual site limits, tested for depth and stratigraphy, and were marked with permanent datum points so the sites could be relocated in the future. The collected sites in the end, however, furnished at least one representative of each site type established for Brantley Reservoir. These collections provide the opportunity to test the adequacy of the models set up from inventory data on the basis of actual counts of surface materials and to revise the models in light of factors not previously considered.

Model Revisions

The percent frequency graph of the surface collections (fig. 15) when compared with the surface inventory record (Table 3) can be very misleading. First, the two frequencies represent different things: the surface inventory represents the frequency of *sites* in each class in which an artifact type was recorded (present, absent); the grab collections represent the combined frequencies of all *artifacts* (except lithic debris and burned rock) recorded from the sites that were surface collected. Several other factors also would tend to make the two representations of "activities" different. Sites *were not* selected for surface collection by a stratified random sampling design. The small number of collected sites in the artifact scatter (large) and the artifact and burned rock scatter (large) categories distort the frequencies because the assemblages on collected sites are not felt to be entirely representative of the larger class of sites of which these are samples. Individual variation in sites of a certain type may tend to skew the representativeness of the surface collection data in the absence of random sampling of sites within each site type.

It was stated that the artifact frequencies from surface collections (which are continuous variables) were generally similar to the nominal scale frequencies from the inventory survey. There are differences, however, that tend to refute some of the functions previously attributed to some site classes.

Revision: Artifact and Burned Rock Scatters (Large)

Artifact and burned rock scatter (large) sites had a low frequency of chipping activities as indicated by the limited numbers of cores and core reduction products. The site collections showed an unusually large number of cores at artifact and burned rock scatter (large) sites. This can be explained by what seem to be peculiar conditions at one of these sites. The large number of cores may be related to the unusually large amounts of burned rock. Most of the cores are of dolomite which is also the material with which hearths are abundantly lined. Whether many of these dolomite chunks are part of a chipping reduction sequence or are a result of fire spalling is uncertain. They were intentionally chipped; however, the range of functions of the dolomite tools is unknown. In general these cores misrepresent the general impression of artifact and burned rock scatter (large) sites. The comparatively low frequency of manos also is of some interest. This situation may be caused by the general high visibility of these large sites to artifact collectors. All the manos and metates recovered from the two collected artifact and burned rock scatter (large) sites were small fragments.

Revision: Artifact and Burned Rock Scatters (Small)

The surface collection profile of these sites generally conformed to that of the site inventory with core frequency the major deviation from the inventory model. This may indicate that the positioning of these sites with respect to areas of chipped stone procurement and manufacture may be significant in the composition of the site activities. Cores may not have been brought back to these sites for reduction as was suggested in the earlier model, but they may have been selected and processed at other locations and more completely finished tools brought back to the artifact and burned rock scatter (small) campsite. While bifaces are infrequent, point fragments and retouched tools are well represented in the assemblage from these sites. The high incidence of manos in the collections from these sites is anomalous. The presence of manos conformed to expectations; however, their relatively high frequency in this case may be explained by the low visibility of these sites to artifact collectors. Many complete specimens were recovered from these sites.

Revision: Artifact Scatters (Large)

The surface collection material for artifact scatter (large) sites does not conform well to the original model except in the continued absence of ground stone tools. Not even fragments of ground stone tools were recovered upon complete surface collection of one site. The comparatively higher incidence of bifaces and hammerstones in this collection suggests that (1) chipping activities resulting in large amounts of fine debitage were being performed on these sites instead of gross scale chipping and reduction of cores and (2) the functional analogy of bifaces as merely a stage in core reduction and hammerstones as just chipping implements may be in error for this kind of site. Hammerstones may be used for chipped stone manufacture as well as food processing tools. Bifaces should be examined for wear patterns related to use in food processing. On the basis of more thorough and controlled collections, the overall weight of the average core and the nature of functional wear on bifaces and hammerstones may help show variable uses for tools of the same general form.

Revision: Artifact Scatters (Small)

The site inventory model and the surface collection frequencies generally conform for this type of site. The only sizable exception is that bifaces are less apparent in the collections than in the inventory. It is important to note that a fairly large number (14) of these sites were collected. The general conformity of the inventory model to the collection frequencies in this site type is some evidence for the activity model previously presented for

these sites.

DISCUSSION AND COMPARISON OF INVENTORY SURVEY AND COLLECTION LEVELS OF ANALYSIS

The controls involved in formulating the preceding models do not allow any high standards of statistical reliability. In addition it is difficult by any means to support functional inferences in archaeology except by analogy and cautious induction. However, the previous discussions of models and revised models clearly show the differences between the inventory level of data organization and the surface collection level of organization. Both inventory and collection data on site assemblages do allow an ordinal level of data organization. This in turn allows the use of nonparametric statistics for description of site types with respect to the composition of site assemblages.

Table 11 (p. 67) illustrates the intermediate steps in data reduction from raw frequencies to ranked information on assemblage characteristics of the different site types in the inventory and collection phases of research in Brantley Reservoir. In Part B of Table 11 we see that the assemblage characteristics for the inventoried sites have been reduced to probabilities that an artifact of the given class will occur on any site chosen for any given site type. The collection data has, on the other hand, been reduced to the average numbers of artifacts recovered from a site of each type on the basis of the collection sample. This information has been derived from Table 8 with the exception of the use of multipliers in sites that were not entirely surface collected. The collection figures form a model of the average number of artifacts predicted from a site in each site type category. Both the collection and inventory assemblages can be ranked in this way. The inventory data is a measure of probabilities of artifact presence on a site; the collection data is a measure of the number of artifacts predicted in each assemblage class on a site of each type.

The first question of interest, having reduced the data in this manner, is whether the assemblages of the various site types really differ from each other. We can measure this in terms of an ordinal scale of "importance." That is, if the ranks of the assemblage traits correlate not at all or negatively between different site types, then it would appear that these site types are significantly different. If on the other hand the rank correlations between pairs of site types are high, then we must entertain the hypothesis that the site types are not different with respect to the ordering of traits in their assemblages.

The statistic used to make these comparisons is Kendall's Coefficient of Concordance. An excellent and readable account of the advantages of this statistic over other similar nonparametric measures can be found in Kendall (1948). Ranking the quantities given in part B of Table 11 we obtain the ordering shown in Table 12 (p. 68). It is fairly clear from this table that lithic debris, and probably cores also, tend to unfairly raise the correlation of site types. In fact it can be shown that the high correlations tend to degenerate as assemblage characteristics are eliminated. The correlation matrix for collection data with all nine assemblage categories included is shown in Table 13 (p. 68). The results of reducing the correlation to 7 assemblage categories, eliminating lithic debris and then cores, are shown in Table 14 (p. 69).

The correlations continue to degenerate as assemblage categories are eliminated in roughly this order: lithic debris, cores, retouched pieces, ceramics, projectile points, bifaces, hammerstones, manos, metates. In a sense then we have created a hypothetical model of the importance or rank of occurrence of assemblage items in the reservoir sites as a whole. As can be seen in referring again to Table 12, no site type in the inventory or collection universes matches this model of the overall reservoir assemblage rankings. The points at which these assemblages for each site type differ in this scale of "artifact importance" serve to emphasize the variability in site assemblages which we have previously tied to functional models and revisions of these models.

A question of interest becomes, then, how closely does the surface collection data parallel the surface inventory data in this quantitative expression of the similarity of sites. To test this it should be asked how well the surface inventory of assemblage importance of artifact classes predict the collection results. If we run coefficients of concordance (Kendall's Tau) between the inventory data and the collection data we should expect the concordance of each site type in the inventory sample to be greater with the same site type in the collection sample than with any other site type (see Table 15, p. 69).

Lithic debris has been eliminated from these calculations because as was seen earlier it only serves to artificially raise correlations since it seems to have diagnostically the highest rank in the assemblage of any given prehistoric archaeological site in this area regardless of type. Reading across this table (rowwise) the odd numbers are inventory sites, the even numbers are collection sites. The highest coefficient of concordance in any given row is the site type best predicted in that column by a site in that row. So, artifact and burned rock scatters (small) – row 1 on the table – in the inventory form the best predictor of the assemblage ranks for artifact and burned rock scatters (large) in the collection ranking of the assemblage ($\tau = .8571$). The inventory rankings for artifact and burned rock scatter (small) sites also closely predicts the collection rankings for artifact and burned rock scatter (large) sites ($\tau = .6910$). This would indicate that the ability to discriminate between artifact and burned rock scatter (large) sites and artifact and burned rock scatter (small) sites on the basis of the rankings of the respective assemblages from the inventory would not be great.

A thorough examination of the correlation matrix (Table 15) shows that the predictions of artifact assemblage rankings from the inventory to the collection of sites of the same type is not always the highest correlation. For instance the inventory rankings for artifact scatter (small) sites is a better predictor of the rankings of the assemblage for the collection of artifact scatter (large) sites (τ = .7926) than for the collection of artifact scatter (small) sites (τ = .6671). All this serves to illustrate the vagaries of comparing poorly controlled observations on site inventories with small sample sizes of site collections, if not the general inadequacy of the site typology system proposed. However, I feel quite strongly that a more careful control of inventory observations and a more fairly chosen sample of sites of each site type would do much to improve the predictive capabilities of the inventory data. Certainly additional tests of such a nature as presented here would be valuable in other regions. In addition collection and excavation of sites in the Brantley Reservoir in the future can be used to test this model of site types and assemblage composition.

As a further test of site type differences, flakes for each of the site types in the collection sample were compared for the presence of cortex on the dorsal surface. The presence of cortex on flaked debris was recorded from the site collections and percent frequencies are shown in Table 16 (p. 70).

The large percentage of cortex flakes on artifact and burned rock scatter (small) sites tends to refute the hypothesized activity pattern on these sites as a simply more limited version of the pattern on artifact and burned rock scatter (large) sites. The Mescalero analogy to artifact and burned rock scatter (small) sites is that they were nuclear family campsites for some specific exploitative purpose that required a maximally dispersed settlement pattern, e.g. antelope hunting (Basehart 1960: 15-19). The presence of both ground stone tools and a range of other tools supports the similarities of artifact and burned rock scatter (small) sites to artifact and burned rock scatter (large) sites. The relationship of opposite extremes in cortex categories of chipping debitage on artifact and burned rock scatter (large) and artifact and burned rock scatter (small) sites, however, suggests the possibility of differences in activity on different types of campsites. This might be functionally tied to a dispersed versus an agglomerated pattern needed to maximize resource utilization. The dispersed pattern relies on locally gathered lithic resources while the agglomerated one relies on materials already selected and modified some distance from camp.

The hypothesized division of function among artifact scatter (small) sites is (1) raw material gathering areas and (2) processing areas. This dichotomy would serve to explain the uncharacteristic debitage pattern found in these sites when the two functional types are lumped together. Finally, the large number of cores recorded from the artifact and burned rock scatter (large) sites which was discussed previously as anomalous must be considered even more skeptically with the great frequency of interior flakes also occuring on these sites. This may simply reflect the intensity and full manufacture of complete tools on these sites with all stages in the manufacturing process equally represented.

Some progress has been made in describing the sites and in indicating possible differences in function as well as structure. It is difficult to verify any of the suggestions made regarding function at this time. However, operationalizing the ethnographic model and more complete and better quality information through testing and excavation should help to clarify, expand, or reject the suggestions made.

TABLE 7
Site Traits from Brantley Reservoir Inventory Survey

	Location	Estimated Size (in sq m)	Estimated No. Lithic Debris	Cores	Retouched Pieces	Bifaces	Points	Hammerstones	Manos	Metates	Brownware	Black-on-white Ware	Other Types	Mussel Shell	Temporal Period ☆
Artifact/Burned Rock Scatter (Large)															
Mortar Holes Present															
X29ED87	R	20,800	1,000	†					†		†			†	C
Ring Midden															
X29ED6	R	12,500	1,500	†	†	†		†			†	†	†		C
Mounds															
X29ED4/5	R	1,031	†				†				†				U
X29ED22	R	700	1,000	†			†	†			†			†	C
X29ED34	R	30,625	1,500					†	†		†			†	C
Scatters															
X29ED10/11	R	6,240	†			†	†	†	†						U
X29ED13	R	193,600	†												U
X29ED17	B	8,250	†	†				†	†						U
X29ED28	R	45,000	350	†			†	†	†			†		†	C
X29ED35	R	40,000	1,000,000	†	†	†		†	†		†				C
X29ED36	R	14,000	10,000	†							†			†	C
X29ED39	R	18,750	100,000	†		†		†	†		†				C
X29ED40/41	R	33,500	100,800	†	†				†		†				C
X29ED45	R	5,000	750	†								†			C
X29ED49	R	8,400	20,000	†	†						†	†			C
X29ED53	R	5,500	10,000	†	†		†							†	U

TABLE 7 (Cont.)

	Location	Estimated Size (in sq m)	Estimated No. Lithic Debris	Lithic Assemblage							Ceramic Assemblage			Mussel Shell	Temporal Period ☆
				Cores	Retouched Pieces	Bifaces	Points	Hammerstones	Manos	Metates	Brownware	Black-on-white Ware	Other Types		
X29ED54	R	10,000	5,000	†	†				†					†	U
X29ED56	R	98,400	140,000	†	†	†	†	†	†	†	†			†	C/A
X29ED57	R	3,200	250	†	†	†	†					†		†	C/A
X29ED58	R	12,000	3,000	†							†	†	†	†	C
X29ED66	B	87,400	1,500	†	†	†	†							†	C/A/P
Artifact Scatters (Large)															
X29ED63	B	55,100	1,543	†		†	†	†			†	†			C/A
X29ED69	B	14,000	100		†		†								A
X29ED70	B	95,140	5,000	†	†		†	†			†	†	†		C
Artifact/Burned Rock Scatters (Small)															
X29ED1	R	555	†								†				C
X29ED8	R	840	550	†	†			†						†	U
X29ED9	R	1,748	15	†											U
X29ED16	B	9	†	†											U
X29ED18	B	300	†	†				†							C
X29ED19	B	200	†	†				†							C
X29ED20	B	975	200	†		†	†	†							C
X29ED21	B	375	†	†											U
X29ED23	R	12,300	92	†	†	†		†	†					†	U
X29ED24	R	3,600	500		†	†		†			†				C
X29ED25	R	200	?												U
X29ED33	R	9,600	†		†							†			C
X29ED38	R	1,000	12	†	†	†									U
X29ED42	R	1,425	35	†				†							U
X29ED44	R	5,300	146	†	†	†	†	†	†						C
X29ED47	R	5,000	250	†	†										U
X29ED48	R	100	500	†											U
X29ED52	R	66	†								†				U
X29ED60	R	1,600	500		†						†				C
X29ED78	B	16,700	210	†	†	†	†								C
X29ED85	R	4,875	100	†	†				†					†	U

TABLE 7 (Cont.)

	Location	Estimated Size (in sq m)	Estimated No. Lithic Debris	Lithic Assemblage							Ceramic Assemblage			Mussel Shell	Temporal Period ☆
				Cores	Retouched Pieces	Bifaces	Points	Hammerstones	Manos	Metates	Brownware	Black-on-white Ware	Other Types		
X29ED86	R	5,900	182	†	†	†	†	†			†	†			C/A
X29ED90	R	2,500	1												U
X29ED91	R	15,000	10				†								U

Artifact Scatters (Small)

	Location	Estimated Size (in sq m)	Estimated No. Lithic Debris	Cores	Retouched Pieces	Bifaces	Points	Hammerstones	Manos	Metates	Brownware	Black-on-white Ware	Other Types	Mussel Shell	Temporal Period ☆
X29ED3	B	300	†												A
X29ED14	B	6,200	70	†	†	†	†	†							P
X29ED15	B	25	†					†							U
X29ED27	R	19,700	40		†	†		†	†		†	†	†		C
X29ED29	B	2,500	200												U
X29ED30	B	3,750	500	†		†									U
X29ED31	B	875	30	†		†		†							U
X29ED32	B	2,500	500	†	†										U
X29ED43	R	15,500	22	†	†		†	†			†	†		†	C
X29ED59	B	4,000	300	†											U
X29ED62	B	4,700	32	†	†		†								U
X29ED65	B	11,000	29	†	†						†				C/A
X29ED67	B	17,000	250	†		†	†	†				†			C
X29ED68	B	400	7	†											U
X29ED71	B	7,300	300	†	†	†	†				†	†			C/P
X29ED72	B	6,000	157	†	†	†	†								C/A/P
X29ED74	B	4,600	35	†	†	†									U
X29ED75	B	20,400	1,500	†			†	†							U
X29ED76	B	2,100	500	†		†	†								P
X29ED77	B	2,800	50												U
X29ED79	B	1,000	500	†	†										U
X29ED80	B	100	10		†										U
X29ED81	B	300	100	†	†		†								P
X29ED82	B	450	25												U
X29ED83	B	9,600	500	†	†	†									U
X29ED84	B	1,800	200	†		†									U
X29ED88	R	1,225	33	†							†				C
X29ED89	R	425	47	†			†								U
X29ED92	B	600	4			†									U

† Present B–Bluff R–River ☆ C–Ceramic A–Archaic P–Paleo-Indian

TABLE 8a
Site Characteristics from Brantley Reservoir Surface Collections

Sites Collected† (Size of site/sq m)	Approx. No. Hearth Concentrations	Wt. of Burned Rock from Area Collected (lbs)	Lithic Debris	Cores	Bifaces	Points	Retouched Pieces	Hammerstones	Manos	Metates	Brownware Sherds	Black-on-white Sherds	Shell Fragments	Bone
Artifact/Burned Rock Scatters (Large)														
X29ED56 (186,000)	86	3,655	2,771	208	9	7	53	3	4	4	7	0	80	1
X29ED66 (87,400)	14	1,638	507	15	11	12	21	1	1	0	0	0	0	0
Artifact Scatters (Large)														
X29ED63 (55,100)	0	0	1,553	84	34	18	54	2	0	0	13	4	0	0
Artifact/Burned Rock Scatters (Small)														
X29ED38 (1,000)	?	78	12	0	0	1	1	0	0	0	0	0	0	0
X29ED42 (1,425)	?	340	35	3	0	0	0	0	2	0	0	0	0	0
X29ED44 (5,300)	?	437	146	41	0	1	2	0	3	0	0	0	0	0
X29ED78 (16,700)	?	78	210	12	2	3	1	0	0	0	0	0	0	0
X29ED86 (5,900)	?	346	172	25	0	2	17	0	10	0	5	12	0	0
Artifact Scatters (Small)														
X29ED14 (6,200)	0	0	70	5	4	1	2	1	0	0	0	0	0	0
X29ED20 (975)	0	0	332	12	1	1	6	0	1	0	0	0	0	0

TABLE 8a (Cont.)

Assemblage Characteristics

Sites Collected† (Size of site/sq m)	Approx. No. Hearth Concentrations	Wt. of Burned Rock from Area Collected (lbs)	Lithic Debris	Cores	Bifaces	Points	Retouched Pieces	Hammerstones	Manos	Metates	Brownware Sherds	Black-on-white Sherds	Shell Fragments	Bone
X29ED23 (12,300)	0	0	92	6	0	1	0	1	1	0	0	0	0	0
X29ED27* (19,700)	0	0	23	13	1	0	1	0	0	0	5	57	0	0
X29ED31 (875)	0	0	30	0	2	0	1	2	0	0	0	0	0	0
X29ED43 (15,500)	0	0	22	17	0	0	1	1	0	0	3	2	0	0
X29ED62 (4,700)	0	0	34	3	3	0	6	0	0	0	0	0	0	0
X29ED65 (1,100)	0	0	26	1	0	0	0	0	0	0	1	0	0	0
X29ED68 (400)	0	0	7	1	0	0	1	0	0	0	0	0	0	0
X29ED71 (7,300)	0	0	300	19	3	1	15	0	0	0	0	0	0	0
X29ED72 (6,000)	0	0	156	12	0	0	22	2	0	0	0	0	0	0
X29ED74 (4,600)	0	0	28	2	1	0	1	0	0	0	0	0	0	0
X29ED88 (1,225)	0	0	33	3	0	0	0	0	0	0	12	0	0	0
X29ED89 (425)	0	0	49	3	0	0	0	4	0	0	0	0	0	0

*Also, 9 sherds of Three Rivers Red on Terracotta.

†All sites were 100% surface collected, except for X29ED56 (1%) and X29ED66 (50%).

TABLE 8b
Classification of Lithic Debris by Material Type
from Surface Collections

Sites Collected	Debris Materials	Flakes				Chips			
		Primary	Secondary	Interior	Biface Thinning	Primary	Secondary	Interior	Shatter
Artifact/Burned Rock Scatters (Large)									
X29ED56	Chert	8	177	599	0	1	167	357	0
	Quartzite	3	24	80	0	1	19	103	0
	Dolomite	12	120	475	0	8	119	376	0
	Other	1	18	51	0	7	12	33	0
X29ED66	Chert	0	59	127	7	2	66	176	19
	Quartzite	0	7	38	0	0	12	20	1
	Other	9	5	11	1	0	1	5	1
Artifact Scatter (Large)									
X29ED63	Chert	29	192	443	16	2	32	72	100
	Quartzite	12	70	182	0	7	38	100	1
	Other	9	42	110	0	3	27	53	13
Artifact/Burned Rock Scatters (Small)									
X29ED38	Chert	0	2	4	0	0	0	0	0
	Dolomite	1	0	0	0	0	0	0	0
	Other	0	0	0	0	0	0	0	5
X29ED42	Chert	0	32	0	0	0	0	0	0
	Quartzite	0	1	0	0	0	0	0	0
	Dolomite	1	1	0	0	0	0	0	0
X29ED44	Chert	1	42	31	0	1	24	17	0
	Quartzite	0	0	0	0	0	0	1	0
	Dolomite	0	4	1	0	0	9	7	0
	Other	0	3	1	0	0	0	4	0
X29ED78	Chert	0	96	23	0	0	10	13	0
	Quartzite	4	18	28	0	0	5	6	0
	Dolomite	0	0	3	0	0	1	3	0
X29ED86	Chert	3	13	33	0	2	15	25	0
	Quartzite	3	15	6	0	0	9	8	0
	Other	1	7	7	0	0	15	10	0
Artifact Scatters (Small)									
X29ED14	Chert	0	11	30	0	0	3	8	0
	Quartzite	0	3	6	0	0	0	0	0
	Other	0	3	2	0	0	1	3	0

X29ED20	Chert	5	23	49	2	2	10	32	18
	Quartzite	3	13	64	4	6	10	29	5
	Dolomite	2	2	9	0	0	0	5	0
	Other	3	5	18	0	0	2	11	0
X29ED23	Chert	0	18	23	0	2	8	8	0
	Quartzite	0	4	4	0	0	0	1	14
	Dolomite	0	3	3	0	0	1	0	0
	Other	0	3	0	0	0	0	0	0
X29ED27	Chert	1	4	17	0	0	0	0	0
	Dolomite	0	1	0	0	0	0	0	0
X29ED31	Chert	1	6	2	0	0	9	3	0
	Quartzite	1	1	0	0	0	0	1	0
	Dolomite	0	0	0	0	0	0	1	0
	Other	0	1	0	0	1	1	2	0
X29ED43	Chert	1	7	4	0	0	0	2	0
	Quartzite	1	0	0	0	0	0	1	0
	Dolomite	0	5	0	0	0	0	1	0
X29ED62	Chert	2	3	8	0	0	0	0	0
	Quartzite	2	6	6	0	0	0	0	0
	Dolomite	2	1	0	0	0	0	0	0
	Other	0	0	0	0	0	0	0	4
X29ED65	Chert	0	2	8	0	0	0	0	0
	Quartzite	5	1	6	0	0	0	0	0
	Dolomite	1	0	0	0	0	0	0	0
	Other	0	0	0	0	0	0	0	3
X29ED68	Quartzite	0	3	0	0	0	3	1	0
X29ED71	Chert	0	23	47	0	1	2	33	0
	Quartzite	10	15	78	0	1	10	16	6
	Other	3	13	15	0	0	8	19	0
X29ED72	Chert	0	15	23	0	0	5	5	0
	Quartzite	2	28	21	0	0	18	23	0
	Other	6	0	2	0	0	3	5	0
X29ED74	Chert	0	8	9	0	0	0	0	0
	Quartzite	1	3	7	0	0	0	0	0
X29ED88	Chert	0	12	8	0	0	6	4	0
	Quartzite	0	0	0	0	0	0	1	0
	Other	0	1	0	0	0	1	0	0
X29ED89	Chert	0	11	13	0	0	9	7	0
	Quartzite	0	3	5	0	0	0	0	0
	Other	0	0	0	0	0	1	0	0

TABLE 9
Nearest Neighbor Statistics
for Various Prehistoric Site Types

Site Type	Number of Sites	Average Distance to Nearest Neighbor (km)	R (Nearest Neighbor Statistic)
Artifact/Burned Rock Scatter (Large)	21	1.33	1.09
Artifact/Burned Rock Scatter (Small)	24	1.15	1.04
Artifact Scatter (Large)	3	1.46	.26
Artifact Scatter (Small)	29	1.04	1.02

TABLE 10
Nearest Neighbor Statistics for Selected Hypotheses Tests
about Prehistoric Site Spatial Arrangements

	Mean distance among (km)		Mean distance between (km)	
Hypothesis 1	Artifact/Burned Rock Scatter (Large) Sites	1.33	Artifact/Burned Rock Scatter (Large) and Artifact/Burned Rock Scatter (Small) Sites	1.33
Hypothesis 2	Artifact/Burned Rock Scatter (Large) Sites	1.33	Artifact/Burned Rock Scatter (Large) and Artifact Scatter (Small) Sites	.68
Hypothesis 3	Artifact/Burned Rock Scatter (Small) Sites	1.15	Artifact/Burned Rock Scatter (Small) and Artifact Scatter (Small) Sites	1.44

TABLE 11

Ranking of Artifact Presence on Sites for Inventory Survey Sites (Part A)

and

Rankings of Artifact Frequencies for Surface Collected Sites for Each Site Type (Part B)

PART A

	Artifact/Burned Rock Scatters (Small)		Artifact/Burned Rock Scatters (Large)		Artifact Scatters (Small)		Artifact Scatters (Large)	
	Inventoried N=24	Collected N=5	Inventoried N=21	Collected N=2*	Inventoried N=29	Collected N=14*	Inventoried N=3	Collected N=1
Lithic debris	24	581	21	278,114	29	1,203.00	3	1,553
Cores	13	25	17	20,830	21	100.25	2	84
Bifaces	3	2	7	922	13	15.25	1	34
Projectile points	7	7	6	724	6	4.00	3	18
Retouched pieces	12	21	8	4,742	13	52.25	2	42
Hammerstones	4	1	4	302	8	9.50	2	2
Manos	6	15	12	400	2	1.00	0	0
Metates	1	0	7	400	0	0.00	0	0
Ceramics	9	17	14	700	6	109.75	2	17

Inventoried represents total number of sites with this characteristic present. *Collected* represents total number of artifacts collected.

*Samples where at least one site was not completely collected and artifact assemblages were multiplied by the percent of the uncollected proportion of the site.

PART B

	Artifact/Burned Rock Scatters (Small)		Artifact/Burned Rock Scatters (Large)		Artifact Scatters (Small)		Artifact Scatters (Large)	
	Inventoried	Collected	Inventoried	Collected	Inventoried	Collected	Inventoried	Collected
Lithic debris	1.00	116.2	1.00	139,057	1.00	85.85	1.00	1,553
Cores	.54	5.0	.81	1,045	.72	7.16	.67	84
Bifaces	.13	.4	.33	461	.45	1.09	.33	34
Projectile points	.29	1.4	.29	362	.21	.29	1.00	18
Retouched pieces	.50	3.8	.38	2,371	.45	3.73	.67	42
Hammerstones	.17	.2	.19	151	.28	.68	.67	2
Manos	.25	3.0	.57	200	.07	.07	.00	0
Metates	.04	0.0	.33	200	.00	.00	.00	0
Ceramics	.38	3.4	.67	700	.21	7.84	.67	17

Inventoried represents the sample probability of this class of artifact occurring on any given site of this type. *Collected* represents the average calculated number of artifacts of each artifact class found on the collected sample of each site type.

TABLE 12
Ordered Ranks from Table 11

	Inventory				Collection			
	Artifact/ Burned Rock Scatter (Small)	Artifact/ Burned Rock Scatter (Large)	Artifact Scatter (Small)	Artifact Scatter (Large)	Artifact/ Burned Rock Scatter (Small)	Artifact/ Burned Rock Scatter (Large)	Artifact Scatter (Small)	Artifact Scatter (Large)
Lithic Debris	9	9	9	8.5	9	9	9	9
Cores	8	8	8	5.5	8	8	7	8
Retouched Pieces	7	5	6.6	5.5	7	7	6	7
Ceramics	6	7	3.5	5.5	6	6	8	4
Projectile Points	5	2	3.5	8.5	4	4	3	5
Bifaces	2	3.5	6.5	3	3	5	5	6
Hammerstones	3	1	5	5.5	2	1	4	3
Manos	4	6	2	1.5	5	2.5	2	1.5
Metates	1	3.5	1	1.5	1	2.5	1	1.5

TABLE 13
Correlation Matrix of Assemblage* Similarity from Inventory Survey Data

	Artifact Scatters (Large)	Artifact/Burned Rock Scatters (Large)	Artifact/Burned Rock Scatters (Small)	Artifact Scatters (Small)
Artifact Scatters (Large)	1.0000	.7714	.6480	.7043
Artifact/Burned Rock Scatters (Large)		1.0000	.7606	.6111
Artifact/Burned Rock Scatters (Small)			1.0000	.7043
Artifact Scatters (Small)				1.0000

*All assemblage categories included.

TABLE 14

Correlation Matrix of Assemblage Similarity
between Site Types from Inventory Survey Data*

	Artifact Scatter (Large)	Artifact/Burned Rock Scatter (Large)	Artifact/Burned Rock Scatter (Small)	Artifact Scatter (Small)
Artifact Scatter (Large)	1.0000	.6000	.3904	.5855
Artifact/Burned Rock Scatter (Large)		1.0000	.5855	.5855
Artifact/Burned Rock Scatter (Small)			1.0000	.4286
Artifact Scatter (Small)				1.0000

*Lithic debris and core categories eliminated.

TABLE 15

Correlation Matrix Showing Value of Surface Inventory Assemblage
Rank Correlations for Predicting Site Collection Assemblages
for Various Site Types

	1	2	3	4	5	6	7	8
	Inventory ABRS (S)	Collection ABRS(S)	Inventory ABRS(L)	Collection ABRS (L)	Inventory AS(S)	Collection AS(S)	Inventory AS(L)	Collection AS(L)
1	1.0000	.8571	.4728	.6910	.4447	.5000	.4536	.5455
2	.8571	1.0000	.6183	.6910	.4447	.5000	.2887	.5455
3	.4728	.6183	1.0000	.5926	.1887	.4001	−.0840	.2963
4	.6910	.6910	.5926	1.0000	.5661	.6183	.2940	.7037
5	.4447	.4447	.1887	.5661	1.0000	.6671	.2996	.7926
6	.5000	.5000	.4001	.6183	.6671	1.0000	.3712	.6183
7	.4536	.2887	−.0840	.2940	.2996	.3712	1.0000	.4620
8	.5455	.5455	.2963	.7037	.7926	.6183	.4620	1.0000

TABLE 16
Percentages of Lithic Debris Assemblage with Cortex on Dorsal Surface
from Site Collections of Each Site Type

Site Type	Number of Flakes	With Cortex Present on Dorsal Surface (Percentages)	Without Cortex Present on Dorsal Surface (Percentages)
Artifact/Burned Rock Scatter (Large)	1,824	24.3	75.7
Artifact Scatter (Large)	1,105	32.0	68.0
Artifact/Burned Rock Scatter (Small)	369	65.9	34.2
Artifact Scatter (Small)	736	42.3	57.8

CONTROLLED SURFACE COLLECTION
AT THE DOLOMITE DUNES SITE (X29ED56)

NATURE AND DESCRIPTION OF THE SITE

Grid collection of a portion of one site was performed as a part of the survey of Brantley Reservoir. This more detailed study was the only opportunity taken to look at intrasite variability. Examining intrasite variability is a crucial part of reconstructing the functional aspects of the sites in the Brantley Reservoir.

The Dolomite Dunes Site (fig. 16), so named because of tremendous numbers of dolomite cobbles used as cores and hearth linings (fig. 17) and the dunes of fine red sand among which the cultural material is distributed, is not only enormous in size (about 200,000 sq m) but also contained the densest concentration of cultural remains of prehistoric sites in the reservoir area. In the sample section collected (1,800 sq m) representing approximately 1% of the site, more than 8,115 kg of rock were weighed and almost 3,000 pieces of debitage collected (fig. 18).

The site was collected with the idea of using dimensional analysis of variance (Whallon 1973) to summarize and describe the patterning of artifacts. There was some skepticism concerning the ability to determine any culturally distinguishable patterning from this site. The site not only is among a series of sand dunes, but there is some evidence of erosion of the site from flood water action. The site was mapped to include the shape and coverage of dunes and the areas of apparent erosion. After completion of the data analysis, it is clear that the degree of disturbance of these and similar sites from wind and water erosion can be easily overemphasized. The dunes of reddish orange sand are relatively well stabilized by a dense growth of mesquite

and other shrubs. The water erosion also can be overestimated. Although there are several large arroyos present, heavy rainfall this last year (September 1974) altered the surface of the site imperceptibly. The site itself seems to be on a terrace well above the flood level of the Pecos, and water entering the area out of a draw behind the site is diverted to either end of the site where the arroyo action is most obvious. In short the patterning of surface materials does to some extent reflect culturally imposed patterning and not pure "noise" as a result of postoccupation alteration of the site surface.

One further factor argues well for a relatively stable surface. There are approximately 100 identifiable stone-lined hearths on the surface of the site, many of which still show dark carbon stains. Many other hearths have been robbed of their stone as indicated by dish-shaped deposits of carbon. It will not be argued that the problem of determining the extent of "N-transforms" and "C-transforms", as Schiffer and Rathje (1973) have termed them, is resolved for the Dolomite Dunes Site; in fact, this is a problem of major concern considering the frequency of similar sites in like situations in the Middle Pecos.

During this field season we could not verify that the dunes actually covered cultural material. This will be easy to confirm by removing part of one or large portions of the several dunes of the site. However, there is no indication that these dunes do not cover occupation areas. The distribution of cultural materials on the surface is entirely between the dunes.

The problems of working with a possibly deflated site, or at least a floating surface, (Streuver 1968: 144) are myriad. However, the common occurrence of such sites has been increasingly recognized in other areas of the

FIG. 16—Setting and Environment of the Dolomite Dunes Site (X29ED56). Note Mesquite-Covered Sand Dunes on Site.

country (e.g., Davis 1975). Obtaining more information from such sites is also made possible because of techniques for statistically sorting out material (e.g., dimensional and nearest neighbor analyses).

*Temporal Placement
of the Dolomite Dunes Site
(X29ED56)*

The ability to typologically seriate artifact styles within temporal or spatial parameters is not well developed for the Middle Pecos. Many regions in the country have at least one sequence of materials from a long occupied stratigraphically excavated cave, rockshelter, or open site. In the Middle Pecos there is no such "index" site or sequence. If this information were available, more effective site sample selection and successful application of these new techniques would be easier. For this reason it is difficult to date the Dolomite Dunes Site. Radiocarbon dates should be obtainable from hearth fill in future work at the site. Current information from neck widths of projectile points indicates dates from early Archaic to Ceramic periods. Although five small pieces of Jornada Brown were recovered, they hardly can date the entire site. Deflated or floating surface sites have been studied to some extent in New Mexico; results of analysis designed to define functional and activity-related patterns have been disappoint-

ing in many cases (Fitting 1971). In the following discussion, some progress will be made in understanding the site function regardless of the unknown depositional sequence and the generally difficult nature of assuming functional associations in the spatial distribution of artifacts.

METHOD OF COLLECTION

The Dolomite Dunes Site was gridded into 10 x 10 m blocks for mapping purposes. This allowed us to map in sand dunes giving a general picture of the artifact exposure pattern between dunes (fig. 18). A stake was placed in the center of hearths located during mapping. Eighty-six hearths were identified in this manner. Two 30 x 30 m blocks were chosen for grid collection as this size seemed to conform well to the size of artifact distribution areas between major sand dune masses. Each 30 x 30 m block was divided into 2 x 2 m collection units (fig. 19). All visible artifacts in each 2 x 2 m block were collected with the exception of the burned rock which was counted, weighed, and then left in its square of origin. Weighing of burned rock was done with a spring scale and proceeded rapidly. The collection itself was time consuming due to the labeling and numbering schemes utilized; this could be altered by having a regular numbering system for each 30 x 30 m unit and recording burned rock weights and counts on

FIG. 17—Dense Artifact/Burned Rock Scatter at the Dolomite Dunes Site (X29ED56).

the collection bags. Only 450 of the 900 sq m considered for collection proved to have artifacts in them (Table 17, p. 80); the rest were covered by sand dune.

ANALYSIS AND RESULTS

The collection of artifacts from the Dolomite Dunes Site allowed the use of dimensional analysis of variance for recognizing patterning among artifacts (Whallon 1973). The kind of patterning actually being recognized by dimensional analysis is the subject of some debate (Schiffer 1974). The major assumption made is that the proximity and patterning of artifacts is dependent on some unspecified functional or causal relationship. By combining different grid collection sizes, a block size is achieved that has the maximum variance for the variable being investigated. At this maximum point, the variable under examination exhibits the greatest homogeneity of distribution with respect to block size.

It was necessary to use a dummy row and column in each of the two 30 x 30 m grid units investigated in order to satisfy the assumptions of dimensional analysis in the Dolomite Dunes collection. Only four classes of artifacts were recovered in sufficient quantity to be of use at this collection sample size: burned rock weights, lithic debris, cores, and all other chipped and ground stone tools combined. The variances for the different block sizes are presented in Table 18, p. 88.

The block sizes for the highest variance of each variable are indicated in the table. As can be seen, the unit size of greatest variance and homogeneity of distribution is not entirely consistent for the different artifact variables. The greatest difference seems to be between Units A and B. There is more sand dune coverage in Unit A which may partially explain the small block size suggested in this unit. It is proposed that variation in activity in the two units is also a partial explanation of the differences between the two blocks.

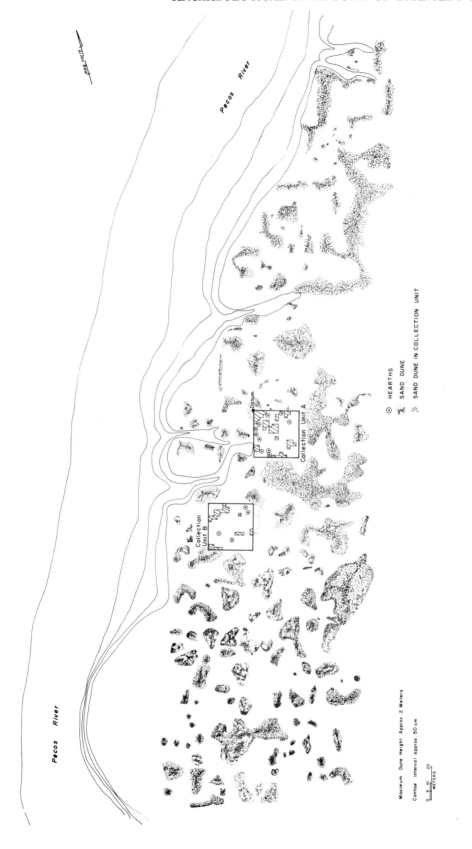

FIG. 18–The Dolomite Dunes Site Map (X29ED56).

Whallon (1973) shows that once the grid size of greatest patterning has been selected, relationships of items can be verified by showing the correlation coefficients of items at various block sizes in the form of correlation matrices. The simple correlations of each artifact type at the 2 x 2 m block size showed no correlations approaching a linear relationship. However, combining all the variables into 8 x 8 m blocks yielded the correlation coefficients (Pearson's ρ) presented in Table 19, p. 88. Although the results are not impressive, the correlation coefficients are raised by combining 2 x 2 m blocks into 8 x 8 m blocks. These data do support a useful approach to the data in their sheer ability to summarize the raw distributional information.

The great advantage of dimensional analysis is that it can be used in grid collections, whereas nearest neighbor analysis provides more accurate descriptive results—but only if each item has been recorded with a unique identifying set of coordinates (Whallon 1974: 16-17). Apparently no statistical method currently exists for nearest neighbor type analysis where data are collected in blocks and more than one item of a class occurs in a block. There is apparently no reliable way of weighting such values or of adjusting for the patterning effects of grid or block collection. This seemed particularly unfortunate in the analysis of material from the Dolomite Dunes Site. Concentrations of burned rock were frequently visible in the form of stone-lined hearths, and it seemed that there would be some sort of artifact patterning around these hearths that might not be visible on the basis of inspection. The hearths suggest a hub or center of activity as an analogy to ethnographic and practical experience. If each hearth did represent a central place around which other activities occurred, this should show up in the average distance of artifacts from the nearest hearth. The average distance each hearth from its nearest neighbor hearth was calculated, and then the average distance

of several classes of artifacts from the nearest hearth was determined. The results of this procedure are not conclusive. The technique used was to calculate the number of squares distant each artifact was from a square with a hearth in it. This artifact/hearth distance was simply the number of 2 x 2 m collection squares between a hearth and an artifact. These mean distances are not straight line distances but are actually biased by the right angle distance that artifacts might be from a hearth. Distances were in 2 m increments because only the square and not the exact coordinates of an artifact within a square were known.

The results of this procedure are best represented diagramatically (fig. 20). The average distance of a hearth from its nearest neighbor hearth is 5.5 m in the sample of 14 hearths within the two 30 x 30 m blocks for which this was calculated. Taking the hearth as a center of activity, average distances of selected artifact classes from the nearest hearth are shown in Table 20, p. 88. Standard deviations have not been calculated. The data are ample to suggest a model of artifact distribution with respect to hearths.

My interpretation of these data generally confirms the intuition that most of the burned rock on the site is in clusters identifiable as hearths. Hearths were on an average about 5.5 m from the next closest hearth while the distribution of burned rock overlapped the average hearth circumference (fig. 20). On first glance the greater dispersion of the rest of the artifacts about each hearth confirms a more homogeneous dispersion of artifacts regardless of the positioning of hearths. It would be useful to check whether artifacts were distributed more closely to some other point or area besides hearths. A random distribution might be shown if the distance of artifacts were closer to points placed randomly with respect to hearths. The manual calculation of distances is rather

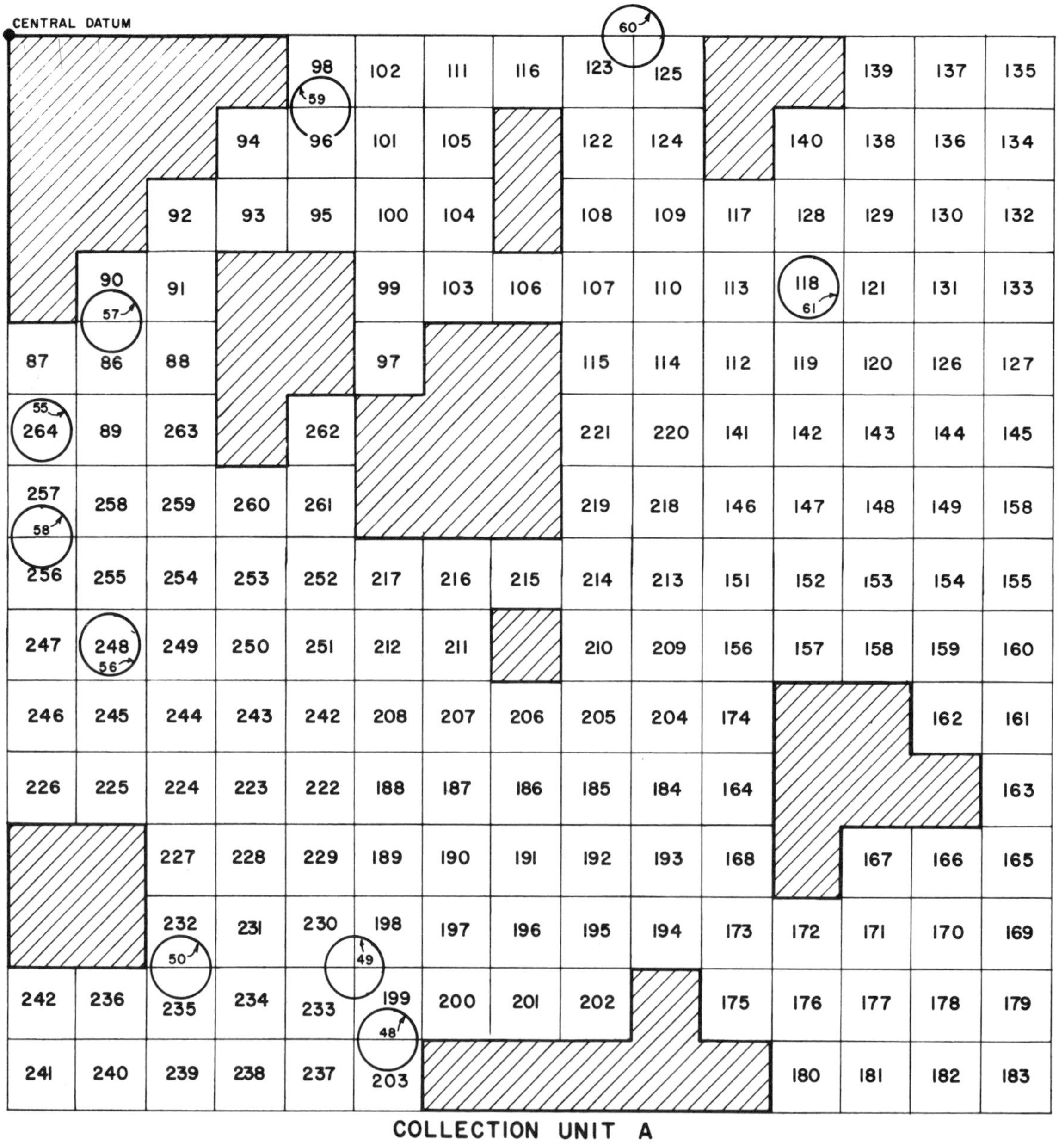

FIG. 19—Surface Collection Units and Hearth Patterns at the Dolomite Dunes Site (X29 ED56).

6OSOW

434	433	432	431	430	///	379	380	381	382	447	446	445 312	465	464
435	436	437	438	439	///	378	377	376	448	449	450	451 36	452
442	441	///	///	///	373	374	375	457	456	455	454	453
443	444	///	429	372	371	370	369	368		458	459	460	461
///	428	427	368	364	365	366	367	266	265	464	463	462
386	385	384	383	362	361	360	359	358	267	268	269	270	271
387	388	389	390	391	353	354	355	356	357	276	275	274	273	272
396	395	394	393	392	347	346	345	344	343	277	278	279	280	281
397	398	399	400	401	348	349	350	351	352	285	284	283	282	///
406	405	404	403 466	402	339	340	341	342	///	///	286	467	///
407	408	409	410	411	337	336	335	334	333	291	290	289	288	287
416	415	414	413	412	328	329	330 338	331	332	292	293	294	295	296
419	420	421	422	423	327	326	325	324	323	301	300	299	298	297
///	426	425	424	318	319	320	321	322	302	303	304	305	306
///	317	316	315	314	313	311	310	309	308	307

COLLECTION UNIT B

mag north

0   2   4
meters

///	SAND DUNE
000	COLLECTION NUMBER
00	HEARTH NUMBER

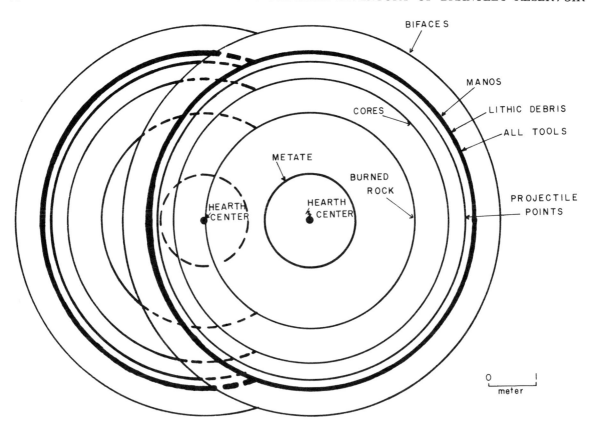

FIG. 20–Model of Artifact Class Distances from Hearths at the Dolomite Dunes Site (X29ED56). The complexity of hearth overlap patterns are shown with the hearth centers placed at the average distance of 5.5 m between nearest neighbors.

tedious, but rapid methods for making this sort of calculation were not available.

Three zones of artifact distribution around hearths are suggested. First, the area in the center of the hearth is composed of burned rock which decreases in quantity as this distance from the center of the hearth is increased. In this zone metate fragments are likely to be encountered. Whether these are discard locations or use locations is uncertain. Since only metate "fragments" were recovered, it seems likely that these were the discard locations. Conversely, why metate fragments were discarded in the hearth and other material discarded away from the hearth is uncertain.

The second zone around the hearths according to this model is a zone relatively free

of debris. This extends from about 5 to 8.5 m from the center of the hearth. These distances are probably expanded somewhat. The fact that one hearth is on the average only 5.5 m away from its nearest neighbor also means that another hearth will be found in the circumference of this zone. This indicates the rather complex overlapping of activity areas visualized on the site. It should be remembered that this is actually only measured to the nearest 2 m because these are calculated on the basis of 2 m collection units. Again, these are not straight line distances but distances which involve right angles. This gives a relative indication of distances, and the rather expanded areas should be compensated for in some way. Some of the heavier waste items, like cores and manos, are at the outside edge of this second zone. Also, the presence of projectile points and other tools within this radius suggests that tools were used or stored here, indicating the predominance of activities occurring in this zone or perhaps that tools were commonly lost in the sand of this area.

Most of the debitage, flakes, and bifaces are located beyond 8.5 meters. This suggests that flakes and bifaces broken in the process of manufacture were either discarded in this area or that the chipping was actually done in separate areas removed from hearths, perhaps to maximize the distance of these waste materials from the heavily used areas closer to the hearths. With more care and larger samples, it might be found that broken tools, food waste, debitage, and most of the garbage ended up in this most distant zone. Although this model is based on very sketchy information, it has the advantage of suggesting a pattern. A few methodological modifications may allow the testing of this model. In addition, this pattern of distribution of artifacts with respect to hearths approaches a consistent formulation of hearth patterns which may be tested on an intersite scale.

Taking both the dimensional analysis of variance information and the modified nearest neighbor analysis done for the two collection units at the Dolomite Dunes Site, several further suggestions can be made about the activities being performed at the site and the general patterning of these activities. Overlays of artifact concentrations showed some patterns that are probably related to the nature of both the dimensional analysis and the modified nearest neighbor analysis performed. Unit B showed less sand dune coverage than Unit A and also a very heavy concentration of debris and other artifacts in the center of the unit which was distant from any noticeable stone-lined hearths. A few black stains were also apparent in this area with lithic debris counts reaching as high as 40 pieces in one 2 x 2 m collection unit. In both units the hearths tended to be at the edges of the 30 x 30 m collection unit. In Unit A there appears to be a semicircle of hearths. Hearths in general appear to occur in sets of two or three, with greater distances between the next closest hearth or set of hearths. The possibility of contemporaneity of sets of hearths or camp circles should not be discarded as an object of investigation. Williams (1974: 107) has suggested that camp patterning of band societies may indicate a great deal about the social structure.

No final conclusion can be drawn about the cultural or natural patterning of the Dolomite Dunes Site. However, investigating the cultural patterning of activity areas has led to a strong case for their measurability. Regardless of the natural forces that have distorted the activity patterns, the occupants who have re-used and distorted previous occupational patterns, and the ravages of recent relic hunters, there is much left of this site that could provide valuable information about prehistoric life at this site and others like it in the Middle Pecos.

TABLE 17

Artifacts in Each Surface Collection Feature at the Dolomite Dunes Site (X29ED56)

Feature No.*	Burned Rock No.	(Wt/lbs)	Lithic Debris	Hammer-stones†/ Cores	Chipped Stone Tools Retouched Pieces (R) Bifaces (B) Scrapers (S) Gravers (G)	Ground Stone Tools Manos (Ma) Metates (Me)	Shell Fragments	Pottery Sherds
86	84	38	19	3			5	
87	0	0	0					
88	34	15	0					
89	0	0	8		B 1		2	
90	0	0	0					
91	24	13	6				1	
92	16	10.5	2					
93	22	9	0	1			3	
94	11	5	2					
95	19	8	0				37	
96	54	34	1				16	
97	1	5	1	1				
98	37	6	2	3	D 1 R 1		5	
99	14	6	0					
100	33	12	1				1	
101	35	10	3	1				
102	0	0	10	1			5	
103	16	2.5	6	1			2	
104	4	.5	0				2	
105	22	4.5	5				5	
106	11	2.5	4		R 1			
107	24	4.5	16					
108	22	5.5	4					
109	33	10.5	9	1				
110	24	7	7	1				
111	8	3	0					
112	22	3	12	1				
113	23	7	11	1				
114	41	7	0	1				
115	15	2.5	16	1		Me 1	2	
116	0	0	11	1	R 1			
117	13	4	3					
118	88	38	2			Me 1		
119	1	2	3					
120	38	16.5	3					
121	28	7	6	1				
122	30	12.5	2					
123	0	0	0					
124	24	8	4					
125	29	9.5	6					
126	19	4.5	14	3	R 1			
127	1	5	1					
128	4	5	0					
129	21	6	1					
130	21	5	7			Ma 1		
131	21	2	4				2	
132	10	2	3				2	
133	11	4.5	10					
134	11	3	2					

TABLE 17 (Cont.)

Feature No.*	Burned Rock No.	Burned Rock (Wt/lbs)	Lithic Debris	Hammer-stones†/ Cores	Chipped Stone Tools Retouched Pieces (R) Bifaces (B) Scrapers (S) Gravers (G)	Ground Stone Tools Manos (Ma) Metates (Me)	Shell Fragments	Pottery Sherds
135	0	0	0					
136	24	6	0					
137	12	4	3					
138	25	8.5	3	2				
139	18	6	1	1				
140	0	0	0					
141	0	0	6					
142	9	1.5	3					
143	7	2	4					
144	4	1.5	1	1				
145	23	4	0					
146	3	.5	2				4	
147	7	2	4				1	
148	10	2	4				1	
149	7	1	7					
150	27	6	2					
151	5	2	1					
152	4	1	3					
153	8	2	5					
154	8	2	2					
155	35	8	7	1				
156	9	1.5	9					
157	5	2	1					
158	8	2	1					
159	11	.5	3					
160	20	8	10					
161	13	3	7	2	G 1			
162	18	12	3	1				
163	23	7	7					
164	9	1.5	2					
165	52	14	0					
166	38	10	4	1				
167	20	6	0					
168	12	3	1					
169	43	8	4					
170	22	8	5					
171	41	13	7					
172	39	13.5	16	1				
173	16	3.5	7	1				
174	7	1	1	1				
175	10	4	4	1				
176	17	1.5	14					
177	38	6	5					
178	29	8	4					
179	51	10	5					
180	18	8	12					
181	12	8	3					
182	4	1	5	1				
183	40	17	0					
184	22	6	3					
185	35	10	8					

TABLE 17 (Cont.)

Feature No.*	Burned Rock No.	(Wt/lbs)	Lithic Debris	Hammer-stones†/ Cores	Chipped Stone Tools Retouched Pieces (R) Bifaces (B) Scrapers (S) Gravers (G)	Ground Stone Tools Manos (Ma) Metates (Me)	Shell Fragments	Pottery Sherds
186	26	13	1					
187	16	5.5	4	1				
188	27	7	3					
189	29	5.5	8					
190	25	8	4					
191	26	8.5	5		R 1			
192	15	5	0					
193	16	5	0					
194	6	10	18				1	
195	22	3	11					
196	15	5.5	2					
197	27	7	0					
198	34	18	4	1				
199	82	51	28	5				
200	27	8	7		R 1			
201	15	5.5	12					
202	4	1.5	2					
203	67	52	1	1				
204	7	.5	3					
205	4	1.5	0					
206	11	4	1					
207	17	5	10					
208	13	7	10	1	D 1			
209	7	1	1					
210	5	2	0					
211	19	7	5					
212	15	3	3				2	
213	12	2	3					
214	2	1	7					
215	4	1	4					
216	1	.5	0					
217	45	8	1					
218	11	3	2				3	
219	18	3	10					
220	7	1	18	1			1	
221	13	4.5	4				3	
222	46	8	12					
223	10	1	6		S 1			
224	2	2	0					
225	0	0	0					
226	0	0	0					
227	0	0	0					
228	46	8	8					
229	10	1	3					
230	36	15.5	0					
231	2	2	9					
232	47	15	0					
233	25	5	4					
234	24	5	5					
235	52	16	1	1				
236	45	13.5	2					

TABLE 17 (Cont.)

Feature No.*	Burned Rock No.	(Wt/lbs)	Lithic Debris	Hammer-stones†/ Cores	Chipped Stone Tools Retouched Pieces (R) Bifaces (B) Scrapers (S) Gravers (G)	Ground Stone Tools Manos (Ma) Metates (Me)	Shell Fragments	Pottery Sherds
237	18	3.5	4					
238	53	10	9					
239	8	1	3	1				
240	46	8	3					
241	31	15	1	1			1	
242	5	1	4					
243	9	2	0					
244	25	9.5	11					
245	60	16.5	6					
246	73	14	10				2	
247	48	15	4	1				
248	140	69	3	1				
249	39	12	4	1				
250	53	19.5	6	1				
251	5	9.5	6					
252	11	4	2					
253	16	2.5	3					
254	3	1	14	1				
255	0	0	3	†1 2	D 1			
256	58	10	3	1				
257	80	25	0	1				
258	35	12.5	6	1				
259	122	17	0	2				
260	12	1	1					
261	17	6.5	1					
262	0	0	0					
263	42	7	10	1				
264	128	20	30					
265	15	9	8	1				
266	13	15	0					
267	37	15	0					
268	102	17	17	1				
269	52	10	79					
270	48	28	13					
271	58	23	0					
272	81	19	16	2				
273	47	16	12					
274*	38	9	1	1				
275	86	26.5	10	1	S 1			
276	16	18.5	0	1	B 1			
277	40	13	0					
278	30	9	15		R 1			
279	0	0	22	1				
280	0	0	13					
281	36	10	1					
282	42	9	11	1				
283	30	3.5	4					
284	3	1	0			Ma 1		
285	6	15	0	1	S 1			
286	11	1	0					

TABLE 17 (Cont.)

Feature No.*	Burned Rock No.	(Wt/lbs)	Lithic Debris	Hammer-stones†/ Cores	Chipped Stone Tools Retouched Pieces (R) Bifaces (B) Scrapers (S) Gravers (G)	Ground Stone Tools Manos (Ma) Metates (Me)	Shell Fragments	Pottery Sherds
287	13	.5	4					
288	17	1.5	7	2	R 2			
289	30	4	17	2				1
290	34	5	0					
291	53	175	4	2				
292	0	0	25					
293	17	3	8					
294	24	3.5	18	2				2
295	2	.5	8					
296	16	3.5	12					
297	18	3.5	15					
298	15	2	15				1	
299	62	10.5	13	3				
300	35	5	4	2				
301	35	31	5	1				
302	35	61	19					
303	22	3.5	11	1				
304	26	2.5	32					
305	30	6.5	32	3		Ma 1		
306	20	5	29		R 1			
307	6	3.5	10					
308	8	2.5	6		B 1 R 1		1	
309	14	3	9					
310	37	15.5	6					
311	64	10	19	1				
312	0	0	0					
313	42	5.5	3	1				
314	17	8	5	1				
315	36	7	1					
316	105	25	2				1	
317	5	1.5	0					
318	79	17	3	1				
319	95	27	5	2				
320	98	17	7	1				
321	66	15	1				1	
322	0	0	1					
323	18	7.5	7				1	
324	52	9.5	3	1				
325	54	13	5	1	S 1			
326	73	16.5	5					
327	112	33.5	7	2				
328	69	9	5					
329	30	10	2					
330	58	55	0			Me 1		
331	58	33	2				1	
332	18	2	6					
333	34	13	7	1				
334	24	45	2	1				
335	42	10	7					
336	50	91	13	2	R 2			
337	46	12	9	2				

TABLE 17 (Cont.)

Feature No.*	Burned Rock No.	Burned Rock (Wt/lbs)	Lithic Debris	Hammer-stones†/ Cores	Chipped Stone Tools Retouched Pieces (R) Bifaces (B) Scrapers (S) Gravers (G)	Ground Stone Tools Manos (Ma) Metates (Me)	Shell Fragments	Pottery Sherds
338	0	0	0					
339	47	8.5	9					
340	70	11.5	12	1				
341	40	4	116	3				
342	22	3.5	1					
343	95	34	29					1
344	85	21	32	2				
345	35	7	11	1				
346	20	2	20					
347	21	3	12	1				
348	45	9.5	0					
349	39	9	6					
350	34	5	4					
351	40	10	6					
352	13	1.5	0					
353	28	7	2		R 1		1	
354	28	4	7	1				
355	40	10	5		R 1			
356	60	28	25	7				
357	75	25.5	27	5	R 1			
358	46	7	54	3				
359	29	9	14	5	S 1 R 1			
360	44	10	26	1				
361	47	12	19					
362	62	21.5	31					
363	42	10.5	7	1				
364	64	14.4	14	1	D 1 R 1			
365	48	10	12	1				
366	45	10	26	2	R 1			
367	33	9	14		D 1			
368	34	13	37	1				
369	64	14.5	6		R 1			
370	16	8	3					
371	25	7	5	1	R 2			
372	0	0	0					
373	46	18	9		R 1			
374	4	1	0	2	R 8			
375	13	2.5	0					
376	43	14	2					
377	46	18	29					
378	20	5	11					
379	8	1	1					
380	17	1.5	4	2				
381	57	13.5	26	1				
382	65	19	9	1				
383	58	81	30	2	D 1 R 1 G 1			
384	87	15.5	15					
385	100	12.5	9					

TABLE 17 (Cont.)

Feature No.*	Burned Rock No.	Burned Rock (Wt/lbs)	Lithic Debris	Hammer-stones†/ Cores	Chipped Stone Tools Retouched Pieces (R) Bifaces (B) Scrapers (S) Gravers (G)	Ground Stone Tools Manos (Ma) Metates (Me)	Shell Fragments	Pottery Sherds
386	0	0	0					
387	29	4	4					
388	31	3.5	0					
389	60	10	15	1	B 1			
390	57	14.5	25	5				
391	34	7.5	18	1 †1	D 1			
392	59	11	9	2		Me 1		
393	43	8.5	18	2				
394	85	15.5	14	4				
395	57	10	8	2			1	
396	40	10	0					
397	33	5	10					
398	75	11	10		B 1			
399	60	10	12	4	R 8			
400	70	9	6				1	
401	74	25	13					
402	70	20	3					
403	79	38	1					
404	50	11	4	1				
405	110	19	22					
406	59	10.5	5	1				
407	99	12.5	7					
408	120	16	7					
409	11	33	7	3				
410	85	21	0					
411	55	19.5	3					
412	120	32	2					
413	78	12	5	B 1				
414	102	16	7					
415	75	11	15	†1	B 1 R 2			
416	76	12	4	3				
417	0	0	0					
418	0	0	0					
419	55	9	6	1				
420	26	15	6	1				
421	90	15	1	4				
422	91	17.5	4					
423	95	17	11	1				
424	41	9.5	7					
425	30	15	2					
426	7	.5	0	1		Ma 1		
427	62	16	1	2				
428	21	3.5	4	2				
429	6	1.5	0					
430	44	12	18	6	R 1			
431	67	10	15	2				
432	60	12	7					
433	50	9	16					
434	31	7	10		B 1			

TABLE 17 (Cont.)

Feature No.*	Burned Rock		Lithic Debris	Hammer-stones†/ Cores	Chipped Stone Tools Retouched Pieces (R) Bifaces (B) Scrapers (S) Gravers (G)	Ground Stone Tools Manos (Ma) Metates (Me)	Shell Fragments	Pottery Sherds
	No.	(Wt/lbs)						
435	55	10.5	8					
436	97	24	0	1				
437	37	7	4	1				
438	32	8.5	15					
439	20	3.5	2		R 1			
440	0	0	0					
441	55	12	3	2				
442	79	14.5	6					
443	50	11.5	10	2	R 1			
444	20	9	0					
445	116	50	7					
446	17	12	22					
447	0	0	20					
448	0	0	2					
449	0	0	11					
450	41	35	0					
451	58	11	11					
452	17	3.5	6					
453	0	0	0					
454	0	0	0					
455	58	30	3					
456	0	0	10					
457	0	0	18					
458	0	0	23					
459	0	0	16					
460	0	0	4					
461	0	0	6					
462	3	1	1					
463	0	0	0					
464	0	0	1					
465	0	0	0					
466	0	0	3					

*Features 1–85 (hearths) not collected.

TABLE 18

Variance at Different Block Sizes
for Four Assemblage Categories
Using Dimensional Analysis of Variance
at the Dolomite Dunes Site (X29ED56)

Collection Unit A

VARIABLES

Block Size	Burned Rock	Lithic Debris	Cores	Tools
2 x 2 m	206.93	7.92	.15	.03
2 x 4 m	206.04	8.83	.21	.03
4 x 4 m	296.65	16.92	.17	.03
4 x 8 m	182.46	14.67	.26	.01
8 x 8 m	*767.01	*32.85	.19	*.05
8 x 16 m	355.46	14.29	.10	.01
16 x 16 m	519.29	15.94	.08	.01
16 x 32 m	225.78	1.22	.11	.02

Collection Unit B

VARIABLES

Block Size	Burned Rock	Lithic Debris	Cores	Tools
2 x 2 m	423.24	23.74	.54	.25
2 x 4 m	86.65	46.18	.56	.65
4 x 4 m	683.86	60.94	.60	.20
4 x 8 m	947.46	48.95	1.08	.21
8 x 8 m	1,305.91	102.66	1.24	*.68
8 x 16 m	2,980.02	254.36	.91	.51
16 x 16 m	*3,501.88	351.81	.43	.24
16 x 32 m	328.23	*496.13	*2.39	.33

*Values with the greatest variance for each artifact class.

TABLE 19

Correlation Coefficients of Artifact Classes
Clustered at 8 x 8 Meter Block Sizes

	Lithic Debris	Cores	Tools	Burned Rock
Lithic Debris	1.00	.71	.65	.55
Cores		1.00	.60	.59
Tools			1.00	.60
Burned Rock				1.00

TABLE 20

Computed Block Distances *of
Artifact Classes from Nearest Hearth

Artifact Class	Distance (m)
Burned Rock	5.42
Lithic Debris	8.66
Cores	7.12
Projectile Points	8.00
Manos	8.50
Metates	2.30
Bifaces	9.76
All Tools	8.50

*Distances calculated are not straight line distances,
 see text.

ANGLO-AMERICAN ARCHAEOLOGY OF THE SEVEN RIVERS AREA

THUMBNAIL HISTORICAL SKETCH

A comprehensive history of southeastern New Mexico is not available. Meinig (1971: 92) nonetheless notes the cultural differences of this area from surrounding areas and examines some of the historical conditions which led to this diversity. At least one amateur historian has considered the Pecos Valley as a suitable unit for historical analysis (Fulton n.d.). The town of Seven Rivers itself has also stirred some specific historical interest (Myers n.d.*b*). Gathering together certain kinds of historical information is essential for adequate evaluation of the historical archaeological remains in the Seven Rivers area. Investigation of local, regional, and state archives for documents relating to Seven Rivers is necessary to adequately understand the material remains encountered in Brantley Reservoir.

The documentary history of the Seven Rivers area begins with early Spanish exploration of the American Southwest. De Sosa passed through the Pecos Valley in the sixteenth century (Sauer 1971; Bolton 1963), but no traces of Spanish or Mexican period material remains were found in the Seven Rivers area. The general situation from initial contact times to the latter half of the nineteenth century in the Seven Rivers area was dominated by aboriginal Indian groups. The general dominance of the Mescaleros in the frontier character of the Seven Rivers area ended about 1870.

In 1866 Oliver Loving and Charles Goodnight moved several thousand head of cattle up the Pecos Valley (Myers n.d.*a*: 7). After this time accounts of settlement and occupation in the Pecos become more numerous, but information is still scattered. Apparently, there were people living in the Seven Rivers area when Loving and Goodnight passed through the area (Myers n.d.*a*: 8), but it was 1870 before a trading post was definitely established with several families moving into the area to settle (Myers n.d.*b*: 4).

By the mid-1870s the frontier ranches and farms of the Pecos Valley were involved in what was to be known as the Lincoln County War. The locality of Seven Rivers is often mentioned in accounts of this civil disturbance. The former Beckwith Ranch, established about 1870 and probably the first ranch in the Seven Rivers area, was a particular focus of dispute at this time (Fulton 1968: 36-43). Documents dealing with the history of Lincoln County have generally focused on the troubles at Lincoln town and the Billy the Kid story. Murders and reprisals seem almost commonplace according to existing documents of the era, especially considering the low population levels.

The community of Seven Rivers owed its development to the dependable water supply, dense grasses, and deep soils of the area. These resources provided good conditions for the movement of cattle up the Pecos River and gave impetus to the development of Seven Rivers. Marginal businesses were established, and Seven Rivers became a local trade center catering to the cattle trade. In 1880 sixteen covered wagons carrying nine families settled at Seven Rivers (Tracy n.d.), and this seems to mark the end of the wilder times in the Seven Rivers area and a shift to a more stable farming/ranching mixed economy. Several of these original settler families still own land in the Seven Rivers area.

Two family histories give some indication of what conditions were like during these times (Ball 1969; Rasch and Myers 1963). These studies indicate that the development of the Seven Rivers community was short-lived and that its demise was rapid. By 1890 there were indications that the stores at Seven Rivers were losing some of the central place functions to the newly founded town of Eddy (now Carlsbad). In 1889 a general election was held in which Seven Rivers and Eddy vied for the possession of the county seat for the newly formed Eddy County. Seven Rivers lost the election. In 1894 the railroad through the Pecos Valley by-passed Seven Rivers (Myers n.d.*a*: 8). The most recent tombstone in the Seven Rivers cemetery dates from 1897, a sure sign that Seven Rivers was dying.

Dam construction on McMillan Dam took place from 1892 to 1894. Instead of creating business for Seven Rivers, this construction led to the shift of economic activities to the area of the dam site. With completion of the dam, Lakewood continued as the business center due to its convenient location on the railroad. From this time on, Lakewood seems to have an economic history not too different from that outlined for Hope, New Mexico (Bulkeley 1966). Although the town had been finally abandoned many years earlier, by 1950 all the old buildings left in Seven Rivers had been salvaged for their stone; and the land was put under cultivation.

ARCHAEOLOGICAL SURVEY OF HISTORICAL REMAINS

The above sketch raises several interesting questions about the area around the historic town of Seven Rivers and about the people and events that took place in the town. It does not really establish an answer to what caused the town to grow and then disappear, nor does it relate these occurrences to a general pattern of development. The archaeological survey raised some additional questions about Seven Rivers.

Historic and recent material remains and refuse were so numerous in the Brantley Reservoir area that it would have been impossible to record every concentration or isolated occurrence of recent artifacts. Beer can dumps,

automobile battery disposal areas, and other refuse heaps were simply too numerous. Some criteria used to identify historic archaeological sites included abandonment of buildings and some evidence of occupation before 1910. With the exception of work at Old Fort Sumner (Wilson 1967, 1968), there are no studies of southeastern New Mexico which examine the material conditions of occupation and habitation in this period. The work at Fort Sumner, however, tells little about the conditions among frontier families and homesteaders in the 1870s, 1880s, and 1890s.

Fourteen historical sites were recorded within the confines of Brantley Reservoir. Eight of these appear to be dwellings (fig. 21); three are apparently well or spring houses; two are dugout sheds; and one is a cemetery (Seven Rivers Cemetery—fig. 22). We believe we have identified the resident families at two of these houses (Table 21). Locating information concerning these families and the families at other sites will aid in explaining the position of Seven Rivers in southeastern New Mexico history. Equally important is the problem of reconstructing similarities in life and economy between family homesteads. These in turn will lead to a broader understanding of the nature of frontier communities and life.

Settlement Pattern

Even the spatial organization of the Seven Rivers community and the surrounding homesteads and farmsteads is in doubt. Photographs in the possession of Lee Myers of Carlsbad suggest that Seven Rivers was a rather dispersed neighborhood of ranches and stores, not unlike the current pattern of settlement in the area. Historic documents that refer to "Seven Rivers" people seem to be in a regional context rather than a central town or community context. The nearest neighbor statistic for historic sites recorded (R=1.30) is not far from what would be expected if the

FIG. 21—Historic Masonry Homestead, X29ED26, in Foreground with More Recently Abandoned Wooden Structure on the Horizon.

TABLE 21
Historic Sites Located Within the Brantley Reservoir Survey

Historic Sites	Estimated Area (sq m)	Structures	Function
X29ED2	1,375	Foundation	Well
X29ED7	1,748	Cemetery	Cemetery
X29ED12	4,690	Foundation	1 House
X29ED13	193,600	Foundation	Well
X29ED26	2,500	Foundation—walls	1 House
X29ED34	5,625	Foundation—walls	2 Houses (Gordon Home)
X29ED37	146	Walls	House (Linger longer house)
X29ED46	9,600	Walls	House
X29ED50	6,000	Foundation	Dwelling
X29ED51	7,000	Foundation	House
X29ED55	3,300	Foundation	Well
X29ED61	60	Foundation	House
X29ED64	575	Dugout	Storage?
X29ED73	2,100	Dugout, corral, foundations	Storage?

sites were randomly distributed. However, this represents a variety of sites with varying functions and does not take account of sites that have been destroyed or disguised by recent land use factors.

Except for the two dugout structures, all

FIG. 22—Tombstone in the Seven Rivers Cemetery—
William Johnson Grave. Johnson was the son-
in-law of John Beckwith who shot him to death
on August 17, 1879.

the historic sites are located on or near the Lakewood Terrace south of McMillan Dam. Evidence for the town of Seven Rivers itself suggests that it was never a tightly clustered group of buildings. There is a plat map drafted for the town in the possession of Lee Myers, but this seems to be a planned rather than actual layout of the town. In patterning, Seven Rivers probably did not look far different than what Fulton (1968) has reconstructed for Lincoln town in 1880. Seven Rivers apparently had several stores and business establishments (Myers n.d.*b*). What or how much was destroyed when the Seven Rivers site was leveled is unknown. Whether the nearby houses which were recorded formed a majority of the community or not is unknown. A photograph of Seven Rivers that must have been taken within a decade of the turn of the century shows only a few buildings in ruins, not a congested civic center.

Population

Population is integrally related to settlement pattern. Myers (n.d.*b*: 6) has suggested that the population of Seven Rivers was as high as 300 in the middle of the 1880s. Obtaining an accurate historical census has thus become a crucial factor. To date we have been able to gather a partial census of 150 names of individuals who probably lived in the Seven Rivers area between 1869 and 1910 (Table 22, p. 94). The research goal is to find additional names of people who lived in the area and to try to establish other demographic features of this population such as land holdings, family size, occupation, origins, and related information. This should provide some concept of activity, economic growth, and settlement patterns in the region. Such information not only will contribute to an understanding of the local frontier history but should provide an opportunity to examine Frederick Jackson Turner's (1920) broader formulation of the significance of the frontier in American life.

Climatic Conditions

The radical changes which have taken place in the ecology of the Seven Rivers area in the last 150 years appear coeval with the first intensive use of the Seven Rivers and Pecos Valley by Americans of European origin. It is not clear what the systematics of this change are. Several climatic fluctuations have occurred in the area in the last 10,000 years. Probably the increase in mesquite, creosote, and tamarisk is due to interaction with human modification of the environment as well as being due to climatic conditions.

Early reports which suggest that prairie grass in the Pecos Valley "could be mowed like hay" indicate an abundance of water. These conditions are apparently not an "ethnic myth", but verification of these conditions on a broad scale has not been obtained. Kiser (1974: 20-21) has gathered information indicating that surface water depletion was beginning in 1882 in the Seven Rivers area. This supposedly raised the need for the development of socially regulated water control systems and in 1888 the founding of the Pecos Valley Irrigation Investment Corporation.

A tree ring chronology extending back to 1655 exists for the Guadalupe Mountains (Schulman 1956). The growth index for this series suggests long-term subnormal growth between 1665 and 1685, with an even more marked period of subnormal growth between 1860 and 1880 (fig. 5). This early period does not conform to drought periods recognized by Zubrow (1974: 11) in the northern Rio Grande. The later period conforms well to drought in California with accompanying population displacements in the 1870s (Meinig 1971: 35). This information is slight demonstration of possible widespread drought in the Southwest at this time. Thorough climatic reconstruction may shed light on this widespread climatic change.

TABLE 22

Partial Census of Residents in the Seven Rivers Area Between 1869 and 1910

1. Rash and Myers (1963)
2. Ball (1969)
3. Seven Rivers Cemetery Tombstone
4. McDonald Cemetery Tombstone
5. Tracy, n.d.
6. Myers, n.d. c
7. Myers, n.d. b
8. Myers, n.d. a
9. Field Notes (Artesia Museum) Dick Detwiler et al 6/25/74
10. Myers, personal communication

Reference No.	NAME/Dates	IN 7 RIVERS AREA (Dates)	OCCUPATION/ RELATIONSHIP	RESIDENCE LOCATION
4	L.F.C.			Buried McDonald Cemetery
4	M.V.C.			Buried McDonald Cemetery
4	Nelson			Buried McDonald Cemetery
4	Joseph I. ?? 1890-95	10/15/1890-1/15/1895		Buried McDonald Cemetery
3	J.C.G. [Gambel or Gordon??]			Buried 7 Rivers Cemetery
3	John W.			Buried 7 Rivers Cemetery
3	J.W.N. [John Northern??]			Buried 7 Rivers Cemetery
3	Andress, "Baby Boy" ??-1893	1893 (d)		Buried 7 Rivers Cemetery
3	Andress, Mertrice Caldonia ??-1893			Buried 7 Rivers Cemetery
3	Andress, Myrtle Zelma ??-1893			Buried 7 Rivers Cemetery
1	Beckwith, Camelia 1857-??		Wife of W.H. Johnson, and later W. Olinger	
1	Beckwith, Helen (Rosalia?) 1863-??			
1,6,7	Beckwith, Hugh (Enrique) 1824-??	1870-1879	Father of 7 children	Lived four miles north of Reed's store, but on east side of Pecos
1,3,5,6,7	Beckwith, John 1855-1879	1870-1879(d)	Son of Hugh & Refugio	Buried 7 Rivers/shot by John Jones
1	Beckwith, Josefina 1860-??			
1	Beckwith, Laura	1879-??		
1	Beckwith, Lorenzo 1893	(Died Infant)		
1	Beckwith, Nicolas P. 1869-??			
1,5,6,7	Beckwith, Robert W. 1850-1878	1870-1878(d)	Postmaster 7 Rivers established 6/19/1877 Born 10/10/1850	
1,7	Beckwith Refugio (Piña) 1831-?	1870??	Dau. of Wm. & Moulda/	8/23/1880 on headstone
3	Bell, Francis 1878-1880	1878-1880(d)		Buried 7 Rivers Cemetery
3	Bell, Moulda		Wife of Wm/Mother of Francis	Buried 7 Rivers Cemetery
3	Bell, William		Husb. of Moulda/Father of Francis	
4	Blevins, William E. 1870-1912			Buried McDonald Cemetery 8/13/1870–5/25/1912
6	Boyle, Andrew			

Reference No.	NAME/Dates	IN 7 RIVERS AREA (Dates)	OCCUPATION/ RELATIONSHIP	RESIDENCE LOCATION
4	Brogdon, Archey 1885-1891			Buried McDonald Cemetery
4	Brogdon, Cleo 1888-1891			Buried McDonald Cemetery
4	Brogdon, H. B. 1865-1920			Buried McDonald Cemetery 12/29/1920
7	Brookshire, "Bob"		Stone Mason in 7 Rivers	
7	Brown, Porter		Saloon Owner	
7	Burditt, Dee		Pharmacist	
5	Burleson, Mrs. (nee Larremore)	1880	Wife of Marion Burleson/sis. of G. Larremore/ came in 1880 wagon train	
5	Burleson, Marion	1880	Husb. of Mrs. (Larremore) Burleson/married	
2	Campbell, Annie		Mr. Larremore's sis./came with 2 wagons in 1880 Friend of Jones Family/later wife of W. M. Jones	
2	Campbell, Jim		Friend of Jones Family	
2	Campbell, Maggie		Friend of Jones Family	
6	Cochran, Tom			
9	Collins, Sam		Founded Holt Cattle Co. 1884	
4	Cook, James C. 1847-1912			Buried McDonald Cemetery 1847– 6/11/1912
4	Cook, Lucinda S. 1859-1901			Buried McDonald Cemetery 1859– 1/11/1901
4	Corn, Livonia F. 1894-1895		Dau. of Peter & Mary	Buried McDonald Cemetery
4	Corn, Mary		Wife of Peter/mother of Livonia	Buried McDonald Cemetery
4,5	Corn, Pete S.	1879–??	Father of Livonia/Arr 1879 with Mart Fanning	Buried McDonald Cemetery
7	Denman	1885–?	Bigoted 7 Rivers land agent	
3	Dow, Infant son of J.L. Dow			
7	Dow, Les		Saloon owner in 7 Rivers/later sheriff	Buried 7 Rivers Cemetery
7	Dunaway, Jerry			
8	Eddy, Charles	1880–1888?	Founder of VVN Ranch/1888–left Pecos area in 1894	
7	Edwards, James R.		Bought cowboy gear 1890	
7	Fannessey, Tom	1869?	Had herd of cattle in 7 Rivers area in 1869/later became foreman of VVN Ranch for Eddy/shot John Northern	
2	Fanning, Elizabeth		Third wife of Sam Jones	
5,7	Fanning, Joseph	1880	Store partner with Robert Pierce/ arr with 1 wagon, 1880/brother of Mrs. Larremore	
4,5	Fanning, M(art) 1855-1913		Preceded 1880 wagon train in 1879	Buried McDonald Cemetery 1/26/1913
4	Fanning, Mary M. 1827-1921			Buried McDonald Cemetery 4/25/1921
5	Gambel, Buster	1880–?	Arr 1880 wagon train/brother of Charlie	
5	Gambel, Charlie	1880–?	Arr 1880 wagon train/brother of Buster	
5,7	Gardiner, Thomas		Small ranch and farm 6 mi west of Reed (1869 or 1870) at the head of north 7 Rivers	
4	Getzwiller, Laura	1882-1911		Buried McDonald Cemetery 2/4/1911

Table 22 (Cont.)

Reference No.	NAME/Dates	IN 7 RIVERS AREA (Dates)	OCCUPATION/RELATIONSHIP	RESIDENCE LOCATION
7	Gordon, Benton		Brother of Carl Gordon/Saloon owner-partner	
7	Gordon, Carl		Brother of Benton Gordon/Saloon owner-partner	
3	Gordon, Catherine L. 1815-1882	?-1882 (d)	Wife of Nelson Gordon. Born 1815 in Batetourt Co. Va.	Buried 7 Rivers Cemetery 7/27/1882
3	Gordon, Faines 1862-1882	?-1882 (d)	Son of Nancy & Carl	Buried 7 Rivers Cemetery 9/10/1882 on headstone
3	Gordon, Jackson 1884-1884	-1884 (d)	Son of Sara & Thomas	Buried 7 Rivers Cemetery-age 1 mo. 5 days/1884 on headstone
2	Gordon, Maggie		Wife of Frank Jones	
2	Gordon, Mandy		Wife of Chas. Jones	
3	Gordon, Nancy		Wife of Carl Gordon	
3	Gordon, Permey	1883 (d)	Dau. of Thos. B. & Sara	Died infant? 7/19/1883
3	Gordon, Sara		Wife of Thomas B./Mother of Permey & Jackson, infant deaths	Buried 7 Rivers Cemetery
3	Gordon, Thomas B.		Husb. of Sara Gordon. Father of Jackson & Permey, infant deaths	Buried 7 Rivers Cemetery
9	Green, Judge Amanias b. Oct. 11, 1824 (Alabama)	1886 moved to 7 Rivers	J. P. for 2 yrs County Commissioner of Lincoln Co.	Buried McDonald Cemetery
7	Harrison, Hank			
4	Hines, Thomas 1836-1898		Drover in 7 Rivers area 1869	
7	Hinkley, James F.	1885-?	Founder of CA Bar Ranch	
5	Henderson, Howard	1880-?	Married Dick Turknett's sister. 2 wagons, 1880 train	
5	Henderson, Mrs. (Howard)	1880-?	Sis. of Dick Turknett/Wife of Howard Henderson. arr 1880 wagon train	
4,9	Howell, J.E.	1902-came to 7 Rivers	Husb. of Viola	Dau. in McDonald Cemetery
4	Howell, "Infant Daughter" 1925?-1925		Dau. of J.E. & Viola	Buried McDonald Cemetery
4,9	Howell, Viola	1902-came to 7 Rivers	Wife of J.E.	Dau. in McDonald Cemetery
2	Jennings, Nancy		Wife of J. Dunaway	
1	Johnson, William Edward Jr.		Son of Camilia Beckwith & Wm. Johnson Sr. b. 4/25/1877	
3,1,6	Johnson, William H. (Sr.)	1875-1879 (d)	Husb. of Camilia Beckwith/shot by Hugh Beckwith/Married Santa Fe 12/25/1875/Ranch with John Wall Wallace Ollinger named J.A.G.	Buried 7 Rivers Cemetery 8/26/1879
2,7	Jones, Barbara (Ma'am)	1878	Wife of Heiskel/Mother of Minnie, James, Charles, Frank, Henry, Sam, William, Tom, Robert, Bruce/Moved into Dick Reed Store, Hotel, Restaurant in 7 Rivers	

Reference No.	NAME/Dates	IN 7 RIVERS AREA (Dates)	OCCUPATION/RELATIONSHIP	RESIDENCE LOCATION
2	Jones, Charles		Son of Heiskel & Barbara/Husb. of Mandy Gordon	
2	Jones, Frank		Son of Heiskel & Barbara/Husb. of Maggie Gordon	
2,7	Jones, Heiskel	1878	Husb. of Barbara Jones (Ma'am)/Children were Minnie, James, Charles, Frank, Henry, Sam, William, Tom, Robert, Bruce	
2	Jones, Henry		Son of Heiskel & Barbara	
2,6	Jones, James		Son of Heiskel & Barbara	
6,7	Jones, John	?1879(d)	Shot by Bob Olinger	
2	Jones, Minnie		Dau. of Heiskel & Barbara	
2	Jones, Robert Bruce		Son of Heiskel & Barbara	
2	Jones, Sam		Husb. of Eliz. Fanning (3rd wife)/Son of Heiskel & Barbara	
2	Jones, Tom		Son of Heiskel & Barbara	
6,7	Jones, William		Son of Heiskel & Barbara/Husb. of Annie Campbell/Saloon operator	Lived ½ mile from 7 Rivers
3,4	Keith, W.S.			Buried 7 Rivers Cemetery
4	Kelley, P.			Buried McDonald Cemetery
5	Krelly, Charles		Mentioned by Tracy "at or near 7 Rivers"	
4,5,6	Kroeger, Paul 1850-1912		One of the earliest 7 Rivers inhabitants	Buried McDonald Cemetery 1850–5/22/1912
4	Larremore, Amanda E. 1854-1905		Wife of R. L. McDonald	Buried McDonald Cemetery 2/10/1854–11/17/1905
3,5	Larremore, George W.	1880	Husb. of Rachel/Father of Minnie/Arrived 1880 train with 3 wagons	Buried 7 Rivers Cemetery
4	Larremore, John 1813-1895			Buried McDonald Cemetery 1813–12/31/1895
3	Larremore, Minnie 188?-1883	1882-1883	Dau. of George W. & Rachel	5/2/188?–12/29/1883 on headstone at 7 Rivers Cemetery
3	Larremore, Rachel 1891-1893		Wife of Geo. W. Larremore/Mother of Minnie	Buried 7 Rivers Cemetery
	Leslin, Frank 1891-1893	1891-1893(d)	Son of J. L. & M. A. Leslin	Buried 7 Rivers Cemetery 7/2/1891–10/3/1893
3	Leslin, J. L.		Father? of Frank Leslin	
3	Leslin, M. A.		Mother? of Frank Leslin	
7	Light, Zack		Les Dow wanted to kill him?	
6	Long, John			
4	McDonald, Elizabeth 1894-1895		Dau. of R. L. & M. E. McDonald	Buried McDonald Cemetery 5/6/1894–2/15/1895
4	McDonald, Mary A. 1885-1886		Dau. of R. L. & M. E. McDonald	Buried McDonald Cemetery 1885–6/9/1886
4	McDonald, M. E.		Mother of Mary, Elizabeth, & William O.	
4	McDonald, R. L.		Father of Mary, Elizabeth, & William O.	

Table 22 (Cont.)

Reference No.	NAME/Dates	IN 7 RIVERS AREA (Dates)	OCCUPATION/RELATIONSHIP	RESIDENCE LOCATION
4	McDonald, R. C. 1875-1931			Buried McDonald Cemetery 2/23/1875–10/12/1931
4	McDonald, William O. 1879-1895		Son of R. L. & M. E. McDonald	Buried McDonald Cemetery 6/9/1879–8/9/1895
4	McGonagill, P. P. W. 1830-1911			Buried McDonald Cemetery 1830-1911
4	Mann, French 1880-1905			Buried McDonald Cemetery
4	Mann, Harrison 1856-1935			Buried McDonald Cemetery 1856-1935
4	Mann, Manale 1855-1931			Buried McDonald Cemetery
9	Merose, Martin		Foreman of VVN Ranch for Chas. Eddy	
4	Murrah, N. A. 1851-1912		Wife of Richard Murrah	Buried McDonald Cemetery 1851-1912
4	Murrah, Richard 1848-1914		Husb. of N. A. Murrah	Buried McDonald Cemetery 1848-1914
6	Nash, Joe		7 Rivers Man in Lincoln County War	
3	Nelson, Clyde 1897-1897	1897(d)	Son of G. F. & S. J. Nelson	Buried 7 Rivers Cemetery 3/24/1897–4/3/1897
3,9	Nelson, G. F.		Husb. of S. J. Nelson/Father? of Clyde Nelson/According to Jim Howell, father of Bill Nelson	
4	Nelson, John H. 1879-1897		Son of W. T. Nelson & Mary E. Fanning Nelson	
4,5	Nelson, Mary E. Fanning		Wife of Wm. T. Nelson/Sis. of Joe Fanning & Mrs. George Larremore	
3	Nelson, Robert 1891-1891	1891		Buried 7 Rivers Cemetery 9/29/1891–12/25/1891
3	Nelson, S. J.		Wife of G. F. Nelson/Mother of Clyde Nelson	
4	Nelson, Thomas W. 1874-1900			Buried McDonald Cemetery 1874–4/2/1900
4,5,9	Nelson, W(illiam) T. 1848-1917	1880-1917(d)	Husb. of Mary E. Fanning Nelson/Arr in 1880 wagon train, 2 wagons/married Mrs. Larremore's sis./According to Jim Howell, resided at 29ED34 houses in 1902 when Howells first came to area	Buried McDonald Cemetery 1848–9/25/1917
7	Northern, John	?–1887(d)	Saloon owner/shot by T. Finnessey	
6,7	Olinger, Bob		Marshall/shot John Jones/cousin of John Beckwith	
5,6	Olinger, Wallace		Second husb. of Camilia Beckwith	
3	O'Neal, G. H. 1810-1887	1887		Buried 7 Rivers Cemetery 10/21/1887
6	Paxton, Lewis			
5	Peril, Ed	1880	Arr 1880 train, 2 wagons	
6	Pierce, Milo		Involved in Lincoln County War	
7	Pierce, Robert H.		Store partner with J. Fanning/bought 7 Rivers store-trading post from Al Rheinboldt	
6	Powell, Buck			

Reference No.	NAME/Dates	IN 7 RIVERS AREA (Dates)	OCCUPATION/ RELATIONSHIP	RESIDENCE LOCATION
3	Prather, Mary Elizabeth 1830-1893	?–1893(d)		Buried 7 Rivers Cemetery
5,7	Reed, Dick	1867 or 1868	First established trading post at 7 Rivers	
2	Rheinboldt, Al		Bought Jones's trading post	
7	Samson, Sam		Ran stage stop and trading post	
4	Sassin, Victor E. 1890-1897			Buried McDonald Cemetery 1890–12/12/1897
4	Segrest, Mrs. A. V. 1854-1886			Buried McDonald Cemetery 1854–7/7/1886
4	Segrest, R(ufe) P. 1840-1916	1869	Herd of cattle in 7 Rivers area in 1869	Buried McDonald Cemetery 1840–11/26/1916
3	Seymour, Eliza L.		First schoolteacher at 7 Rivers	Buried 7 Rivers Cemetery
9	Shattuck, "Captain"			
7	Sheremyer, Fred		Boot and saddle store at 7 Rivers	
4	Sims, Matthew P. 1850-1926		Attacked at Indian Creek	Buried McDonald Cemetery 1850–1926
7	Slaughter, Charlie		Arrived 1880 train, 2 wagons	
5	Turknett, Dick	1880	Trading post	
6	Turner, Marion		Succeeded Bob Beckwith as 7 Rivers postmaster	
2	Upson, Ash		Husb. of Turknett's sis.,/arrived 1880, 1 wagon	
5	Watson, Levi	1880		
5	Watson, Mrs. Levi (Turknett)	1880	Arr. 1880/sis. of Dick Turknett/wife of Levi Watson	
4	Wilbur, H. H.		Father of Roxie	
4	Wilbur, L. B.		Mother of Roxie	
4	Wilbur, Roxie 1907-1911		Dau. of H. H. & L. B.	Buried McDonald Cemetery 1907–1911
5,7	Woods, Jim		Husb. of Rachel Fanning Larremore/blacksmith/ arr with 1 wagon in 1880/married Mrs. Geo. Larremore's sis., Mrs. Rachel Fanning Woods	
5	Woods, Mrs. Rachel Fanning	1880	Sis. of Mrs. Geo. Larremore & Joe Fanning/came to 7 Rivers 1880 wagon train/sis-in-law of J.T. Larremore	

ARCHAEOLOGICAL PROBLEMS AND ARCHAEOLOGICAL POTENTIAL OF THE SEVEN RIVERS AREA

The particular problems which confront the archaeologist in the Middle Pecos Valley can be at least partially answered by further study and excavations in the Brantley Reservoir and Seven Rivers area. Some of these problems have not been touched upon directly as they are small problems compared to general ones about the nature of past settlement and subsistence in the Pecos Valley.

Although a synchronic model of settlement types and functions has been established, I have not touched on the possibly diachronic differences between large scatters of burned rock, sites which have mounds of burned rock, and the single site that is a ring-shaped accumulation of burned rock. These fundamental differences in the distribution of burned rock are perhaps very significant in observing cultural change or functional variation of sites in the Middle Pecos Valley.

Reconstructing the lifeways of the Middle Pecos inhabitants anticipates the general archaeological problem of explaining the operation of cultural systems in the past when available tools are inadequate for explaining the operation of cultural systems existing today. This dilemma should encourage the examination of large and small problems in explaining culture change in any given region, and thus shed some light on understanding human behavior.

ENVIRONMENTAL RECONSTRUCTION

The crucial problem in environmental reconstruction is the testing of Antevs's (1955) chronology of environmental fluctuation as it applies to the Middle Pecos. We have previously gathered many lines of evidence together to suggest that Antevs's postulated fluctuations may be chronologically valid points of climatic change for the Middle Pecos. Developing a representative pollen sequence for the Brantley Reservoir area is a fundamental aspect of reconstructing the environment.

CHRONOLOGICAL PLACEMENT

Developing a chronology of stylistic change in the Seven Rivers area is also of crucial importance. It is unlikely that much progress can be made in estimating rates or degrees of cultural change if no scale exists for measuring this change. The nature of many sites (for example, open blowouts) may seriously hamper efforts of developing a chronology. However, there are many possibilities for obtaining dateable materials in archaeological contexts. Because of the difficulty of obtaining dateable materials in the Middle Pecos, special caution should be taken in utilizing new techniques such as thermoluminescence of ceramics, hydration rates of chipped stone, and archaeomagnetism to date deposits.

SETTLEMENT PATTERNS

A great deal of this report has been concerned with describing the distribution of archaeological sites and with trying to segregate the variability between archaeological sites. There are several levels to this problem.

Can the settlement typology which corresponds to a functional typology of archaeological sites in the Seven Rivers area be verified? Accurate mapping of site dimensions, controlled collection of site assemblages, quantitative analysis of assemblage categories, and relating sites to areas of ecological resources have all been suggested as solutions to the verification of functional relationships.

If the site typology suggested here cannot be verified, it could be due to over-simplification of the already obvious variability between sites of a given type. Artifact and burned rock scatter (large) sites have been treated as a *solidary* unit. There is some obviously significant variation between these sites. Sites with mortarholes, burned rock mounds, ring middens, and quantities of scattered burned rock allow us to further subdivide this site class (fig. 10). Whether these differences are largely related to temporal variation in the utilization of the Seven Rivers area, to local resources, or to yearly fluctuations in resources is unmeasured. There is some suggestion that burned rock mounds precede ring middens, and burned rock scatters precede mounds in a temporal sense (compare dates of Greer 1968*a* and Sommer 1968). Verifying this change and relating it to the social structure involved in creating these different kinds of settlement structures is an important problem that may bear on all of Middle Pecos archaeology.

The high number of sites with ceramics on them suggests the probability that our most complete reconstruction of settlement patterns and activities may come from an analysis of sites that can be tied to the Ceramic time period. Special attention should be paid to the variability of site types in the quantitatively significant numbers of Ceramic period sites. However, if it does become possible to date site assemblages from other periods, we may be able to make similar detailed studies of these periods as well.

Intrasite settlement pattern or activity analysis is also a problem for which analytical tools are available. The Dolomite Dunes Site collection is just one demonstration of these techniques. They should be more rigorously employed on a comparative basis between different sites. The performance of certain activities within certain parameters on different sites should yield a wealth of comparative in-formation. We may not only find that ring middens and burned rock mounds differ in their period of use, but also represent radically different associations of basic activities to the same subsistence materials. This in turn may allow us to speak of social organization within the groups being studied. A great deal of homogeneity is often presumed in the social organization of different hunting and gathering societies. Change in this social organization may be demonstrable within the sequence in the Seven Rivers area.

INFORMATION RETRIEVAL

The Middle Pecos is infested with exposed, "reworked," deflated, and disturbed archaeological remains. A serious problem is assuming that there is some *de facto* organization of the material remains on an open archaeological site when in fact geological, climatic, and ecological processes have been operating to change and distort the patterning. It is necessary to document what kind of disturbing processes have occurred and show explicitly the effect they have on archaeological remains. For example, at the Dolomite Dunes Site, to what extent the nature of the artifact distribution is due to disturbance is uncertain. If some specific techniques were more carefully developed for examining this situation in the Middle Pecos, the archaeology of this region might be less prone to be dismissed as a "lost cause." This seems to have been the motivating attitude for lack of professional interest in this area for some number of years. It has also provided a willful justification for wholesale destruction of archaeological remains by artifact collectors. Demonstrating the degree to which archaeological materials are still in "de facto refuse" (Schiffer 1972:162) situations on open sites is a crucial problem in conserving Middle Pecos archaeological remains.

HISTORICAL ARCHAEOLOGY

The problems of examining historical remains archaeologically are different in some ways from those problems in the prehistoric framework. Many of the same archaeological techniques might be successfully applied. In fact, historic sites might provide a sort of baseline in examining information loss due to environmental and cultural disturbance of sites. However, the historical archaeology is even more complex than the prehistoric archaeology because of the additional records and information sources that can be discovered. Historical archaeology in the Seven Rivers area will provide a rare opportunity to study frontier life in detail. The success of the historical archaeological approach will depend on the success of the "salvage ethnology" done in the reservoir area. There are still a few living memories left of the time period between 1870 and 1910. Detailed studies of frontier communities are very rare from an historical archaeological perspective. We sometimes assume that Americans have lived in much the same way for the past century. In fact, there have been some very radical changes. Historical archaeology at Brantley Reservoir should allow us to appreciate the degree of these changes when combined with the appropriate documentary and ethnographic approach.

ETHNOGRAPHIC ANALOGY

Some time has been spent in constructing an ethnographic model of subsistence and settlement in the Middle Pecos. This model has not been fully operationalized. It functions mostly as a means for keeping in touch with the archaeological goal of reconstructing culture from material remains. By being confronted with actual ethnographic information we must recognize some of the gaps that archaeological methods seem to leave in an understanding of vanished cultural systems. Operationalizing models of cultural systems through ethnographic information "keeps us honest" about our capacities as well as providing new insight into the archaeological record. Turning the Mescalero model of subsistence and settlement presented here into a quantitative simulation of ethnographic patterns will help us better predict archaeological outcomes of subsistence and settlement models for vanished cultures.

These six problem areas have formed the core of this report. Future research in the archaeology at Brantley Reservoir should not only provide a more detailed inventory of the material remains found in the area but should also develop some of the techniques suggested and aim at more complete information on the culture history and better explanation of culture change in the Middle Pecos Valley. A thorough understanding of the past use of this area should enable us all to reasonably evaluate the intelligence of future decisions regarding large- and small-scale modifications which we undertake on this scenic territory.

BIBLIOGRAPHY

ASHBEE, P., and CORNWALL, I. W., 1961. An Experiment in Field Archaeology. Antiquity 35:129-34.

ANTEVS, E., 1955. Geologic-Climatic Dating in the West. American Antiquity 20(4):317-55.

APPLEGARTH, J. S., 1975. Environmental Implications of Herpetofaunal Remains from Archeological Sites West of Carlsbad, New Mexico. Paper presented at Symposium for Biological Investigations in the Guadalupe Mountains National Park, Texas.

AYER, M. Y., 1936. The Archaeological and Faunal Material from Williams Cave, Guadalupe Mountains, Texas. Proceedings of the Academy of Natural Sciences of Philadelphia 88:599-618.

BAILEY, V., 1928. Animal Life of the Carlsbad Cavern. Monographs of the American Society of Mammalogists No. 3.

BALL, E., 1969. Ma'am Jones of the Pecos. Tucson: University of Arizona Press.

BASEHART, H., 1960. Mescalero Apache Subsistence Patterns and Socio-Political Organizations, Section I. A Report of the Mescalero-Chiricahua Land Claims Project. Contract Research No. 290-154, University of New Mexico.

————, 1971. Mescalero Apache Band Organization and Leadership. *In* Apachean Culture History and Ethnology, edited by Keith H. Basso and Morris E. Opler, pp. 35-50. University of Arizona Anthropological Papers No. 21.

BINFORD, L. R., 1967. Smudge Pits and Hide Smoking: The Role of Analogy in Archaeological Reasoning. American Antiquity 32(1):1-12.

BLACK, C. C., (editor), 1974. History and Prehistory of the Lubbock Lake Site. Lubbock: West Texas Museum Association.

BLAIR, F. W., 1950. The Biotic Provinces of Texas. Texas Journal of Science 2(1):93-117.

BOLTON, H. E., 1963. Spanish Exploration in the Southwest 1542-1706. (Originally published in 1908). New York: Barnes and Noble.

BOUSMAN, B., 1974*a*. An Archaeological Assessment of Carlsbad Caverns National Park. Report submitted to the National Park Service by the Archaeology Research Program, Southern Methodist University.

————, 1974*b*. An Archaeological Reconnaissance of Brantley Reservoir. Report prepared by the Archaeology Research Program, Southern Methodist University.

BRADLEY, Z. A., 1959. Cave Site A-08 Carlsbad Caverns. National Park Service Special Report, Carlsbad Caverns National Park.

BRETERNITZ, D., 1966. An Appraisal of Tree-Ring Dated Pottery in the Southwest. Anthropological Papers of the University of Arizona, No. 10.

BRETZ, J. H., and HORBERG, L., 1949. The Ogallala Formation West of the Llano Estacado. Journal of Geology 57:477-90.

BROILO, F., 1973. The Glencoe Project: Archaeological Salvage Investigations Along U.S. Highway 70, Near Ruidoso, Lincoln County, New Mexico. Santa Fe: Laboratory of Anthropology Notes No. 68.

BRYANT, V. M., 1969. Late Full-Glacial and Post-Glacial Pollen Analysis of Texas Sediments. Ph.D. dissertation, University of Texas, Austin. Ann Arbor: Xerox University Microfilms.

BULKELEY, O. R., 1966. Hope, New Mexico: An Experiment with a Locally Operated Community Ditch. Master's thesis, New Mexico State University.

BURNS, B., 1967. The Archaeology of the Carlsbad District, Southeastern New Mexico. Unpublished B.A. thesis, Department of Anthropology, University of Arizona.

————, 1972. A Method for the Location and Recognition of Southwestern Apache Sites. Unpublished manuscript on file at the Arizona State Museum Library, University of Arizona.

CAMPBELL, R. S., 1929. Vegetative Succession in the Prosopis Dunes of Southern New Mexico. Ecology 10:392-98.

CARTER, G. F., 1945. Plant Geography and Culture History in the American Southwest. Viking Fund Publications in Anthropology No. 5.

CASTETTER, E. F., and OPLER, M. E., 1936. The Ethnobiology of the Chiricahua and Mescalero Apache. University of New Mexico Biology Bulletin 4(5):3-63.

COLLINS, M., 1968. The Andrews Lake Locality: New Archaeological Data from the Southern Llano Estacado, Texas. Master's thesis, University of Texas, Austin.

CORLEY, J. A., 1965. Proposed Eastern Extension of the Jornada Branch of the Mogollon. Papers of the Southeastern New Mexico and West Texas Symposium, Vol. 1.

————, and LESLIE, R., 1960. The Boot Hill Site LCAS B-5. Hobbs: Lea County Archaeological Society Bulletin 2.

CORLISS, D. W., 1972. Neck Width of Projectile Points: An Index of Culture Continuity and Change. Occasional Papers of the Idaho State University Museum No. 29.

COSGROVE, C. B., 1947. Caves of the Upper Gila and Hueco Areas in New Mexico and Texas. Cambridge, Mass.: Papers of the Peabody Museum of American Archaeology and Ethnology, Vol. 24, No. 2.

COUES, E., 1895. The Expedition of Zebulon Montgomery Pike (1805-1807). New York: Francis P. Harper.

DAVIS, E. L., 1975. The 'Exposed Archaeology' of China Lake. American Antiquity 40(1):39-54.

DIBBLE, D. S., and LORRAIN, D., 1968. Bonfire Shelter: A Stratified Bison Kill Site, Val Verde County, Texas. Austin: Texas Memorial Museum Miscellaneous Papers No. 1.

DILLEHAY, T. D., 1975. Late Quaternary Bison Population Changes on the Southern Plains. Plains Anthropologist 19(65):180-96.

DUFFIELD, L. F., 1970. Some Panhandle Aspect Sites: Their Vertebrates and Paleoecology. Ph.D. dissertation, University of Wisconsin. Ann Arbor: Xerox University Microfilms.

FERDON, E. N., 1946. Hermit's Cave. Monographs of the School of American Research 10.

FIEDLER, A. G., and NYE, S. S., 1933. Geology and Ground Water Resources of the Roswell Artesian Basin, New Mexico. U.S. Geological Survey Water Supply Paper 639.

FITTING, J. B., 1971. The Burris Ranch Site, Doña Ana County, New Mexico. Case Western Reserve University, Southwestern New Mexico Research Report No. 1.

FULTON, M. G., 1968. Maurice G. Fulton's History of the Lincoln County War, edited by R. N. Mullin. Tucson: University of Arizona Press.

————, n.d. Pecos Valley History. Maurice Garland Fulton Special Collections. Tucson: University of Arizona Library.

GARDNER, J. L., 1950. Effects of Thirty Years of Protection of Grazing in Desert Grassland. Ecology 31(1):44-50.

GEHLBACH, F. R., 1967. Vegetation of the Guadalupe Escarpment, New Mexico–Texas. Ecology 48(3):404-19.

GIFFORD, E. W., 1940. Culture Element Distributions: XII Apache - Pueblo. University of California, Berkeley Anthropological Records 4(1).

GREEN, R. C., 1956. Excavations near Mayhill, New Mexico. *In* Highway Salvage Archaeology II(7), edited by F. Wendorf, pp. 1-9. Santa Fe: New Mexico Highway Department and Museum of New Mexico.

GREER, J., 1965. A Typology of Midden Circles and Mescal Pits. Southwestern Lore 31(3):41-55.

————, 1966. Preliminary Archaeological Explorations at Carlsbad Caverns National Park, New Mexico. Unpublished manuscript, University of Texas, Austin.

————, 1968*a*. Notes on Excavated Ring Midden Sites, 1963-1968. Bulletin of the Texas Archeological Society 38:39-44.

————, 1968*b*. Excavations at a Midden Circle Site in El Paso County, Texas. Bulletin of the Texas Archeological Society 39:111-32.

HAFSTEN, U., 1961. Pleistocene Development of Vegetation and Climate in the Southern High Plains as Evidenced by Pollen Analysis. *In* Paleoecology of the Llano Estacado, edited by F. Wendorf. Fort Burgwin Research Center 1:59-91.

HAGGET, P., 1966. Locational Analysis in Human Geography. New York: St. Martin's Press.

HAMMACK, L. C., 1965. Archaeology of the Ute Dam and Reservoir. Museum of New Mexico Papers in Anthropology No. 14.

HARRINGTON, J. P., 1940. Southern Peripheral Athapaskawan Origins, Divisions, and Migrations. Smithsonian Institution Miscellaneous Collections 100:503-32.

HARRIS, A. H., 1970. The Dry Cave Mammalian Fauna and Late Pluvial Conditions in Southeastern New Mexico. Texas Journal of Science 22(1):3-27.

HARRIS, R., 1966. Recent Plant Invasions in the Arid and Semi-Arid Southwest of the U. S. Annals of the Association of American Geographers 56:408-22.

HAYES, P. T., 1964. Geology of the Guadalupe Mountains, New Mexico. U. S. Geological Survey Professional Paper 446.

HAYNES, C. V., Jr., 1967. Carbon-14 Dates and Early Man in the New World. *In* Pleistocene Extinctions, edited by P. S. Martin and H. E. Wright, Jr. New Haven: Yale University Press.

————, 1975. Pleistocene and Recent Stratigraphy. *In* Late Pleistocene Environments of the Southern High Plains, edited by F. Wendorf and J. Hester, pp. 57-96. Fort Burgwin Research Center Publication No. 9.

HENDERSON, E. B., and LEVY, J. E., 1975. Survey of Navajo Community Studies 1936-1974. Lake Powell Research Project Bulletin No. 6. Department of Anthropology, University of Arizona.

HONEA, K., 1973. The Technology of Eastern Puebloan Pottery on the Llano Estacado. Plains Anthropologist 18:73-88.

HORBERG, L., 1949. Geomorphic History of the Carlsbad Caverns Area, New Mexico. Journal of Geology 57:7-26.

HOWARD, E. B., 1930. Archaeological Research in the Guadalupe Mountains. Museum of the University of Pennsylvania Museum Journal 21(3-4):180-213.

————, 1935. Evidence of Early Man in North America. University of Pennsylvania Museum Journal 24(2-3):61-175.

HUMAN SYSTEMS RESEARCH, 1972. Training Bulletin. Tularosa Valley Project, 1972 Excavations at Fresnal Shelter. Human Systems Research.

————, 1973. Technical Manual: Human Systems Research. Human Systems Research.

JAEGER, E. C., 1957. The North American Deserts. Stanford: Stanford University Press.

JELINEK, A. J., 1967. A Prehistoric Sequence in the Middle Pecos Valley, New Mexico. University of Michigan Museum of Anthropology, Anthropological Paper No. 31.

JENNINGS, J. D., 1940. A Variation of Southwestern Pueblo Culture. Laboratory of Anthropology Technical Series Bulletin 10.

JUDGE, W. J., 1973. Paleo-Indian Occupation of the Central Rio Grande Valley in New Mexico. Albuquerque: University of New Mexico Press.

_____, 1974. The Excavation of Tijeras Pueblo 1971-1973: Preliminary Report Cibola National Forest, New Mexico. Albuquerque: U. S. Department of Agriculture Forest Service.

KATZ, S. R., and KATZ, P. R., 1974. An Inventory and Interpretation of Prehistoric Resources in Guadalupe Mountains National Park, Texas. Report submitted to the National Park Service by Texas Tech University.

KELEHER, W. A., 1959. Violence in Lincoln County 1869-1881. Albuquerque: University of New Mexico Press.

KELLEY, J. H., 1966. The Archaeology of the Sierra Blanca Region of Southeastern New Mexico. Ph.D. dissertation, Harvard University.

KELLEY, V. C., 1971. Geology of the Pecos Country, Southeastern New Mexico. New Mexico Bureau of Mines and Mineral Resources Memoir 24.

KENDALL, M. G., 1948. Rank Correlation Methods. London: Charles Griffin and Co., Ltd.

KIDDER, A. V., 1924. An Introduction to the Study of Southwestern Archaeology with a Preliminary Account of the Excavation at Pecos. Phillips Academy Papers of the Southwestern Expedition No. 1. New Haven: Yale University Press.

KISER, E., 1974. Historical Analysis: Brantley Reservoir Project. Paper on file with the Archaeology Research Program, Southern Methodist University.

KUNZ, M. L., 1969. The Cultural Implications of the Archaeology of Billy the Kid Cave. Transactions of the Fifth Regional Archeological Symposium for Southeastern New Mexico and Western Texas 5:13-23.

_____; GAMACHE, G. L.; and AGOGINO, G., 1973. The Material Culture from Billy the Kid Cave and the Late Cultural History of Blackwater Draw. AWANYU 1(3):38-48.

LeCLAIR, E. E. Jr., 1962. Economic Theory and Economic Anthropology. American Anthropologist 64(6): 1179-1203.

LESLIE, R., 1965. The Merchant Site. Transactions of the First Regional Archeological Symposium for Southeastern New Mexico and Western Texas, pp. 23-29.

_____, 1968. The Monument Spring Site, LCAS No. D16. Transactions of the Fourth Regional Archeological Symposium for Southern New Mexico and Western Texas, pp. 79-83.

MARSHALL, M. P., 1973. Background Information on the Jornada Culture Area. Human Systems Research Technical Manual, 1973.

MARTIN, P. S., 1963. The Last 10,000 Years. Tucson: University of Arizona Press.

_____, 1967. Pollen Analysis of Prehistoric Middens Near Ft. Sumner, New Mexico. *In* A Prehistoric Sequence in the Middle Pecos Valley, New Mexico, by A. J. Jelinek. University of Michigan Museum of Anthropology Papers 31: 130-34.

MEINIG, D. W., 1971. Southwest: Three Peoples in Geographical Change 1600-1970. London: Oxford University Press.

MEINZER, O.E.; RENICK, B.C.; and BRYAN, K., 1927. Contributions to the Hydrology of the United States, 1926: Geology of No. 3 Reservoir Site at the Carlsbad Irrigation Project, New Mexico, with Respect to Water-Tightness. U.S. Geological Survey Water Supply Paper 580, pp. 1-39.

MERA, H. P., 1938. Reconnaissance and Excavations in Southeastern New Mexico. Memoirs of the American Anthropological Association No. 51.

————, 1943. An Outline of Ceramic Development in Southern and Southeastern New Mexico. Laboratory of Anthropology Technical Series 11.

MILLER, J. P., 1958. Problems of the Pleistocene in Cordilleran North America as Related to Recognition of Environmental Changes that Affected Early Man. *In* Climate and Man in the Southwest, edited by T. L. Smiley. University of Arizona Bulletin 28(4):19-49.

MOONEY, J., 1928. The Aboriginal Population of America North of Mexico. Smithsonian Miscellaneous Collections 80(7).

MURRAY, K. F., 1957. Pleistocene Climate and Fauna of Burnet Cave, New Mexico. Ecology 38(1):129-32.

MYERS, L. C., n.d. *a*. Eddy County. . .A Fond Look Back. Artesia: Valley Savings and Loan.

————, n.d. *b*. Pecos Valley Cow Town. Unpublished manuscript.

————, n.d. *c*. Notes before Antique Ladies Division of Carlsbad Women's Club.

NAROLL, R., 1964. On Ethnic Unit Classification. Current Anthropology 5(4):283-312.

————, 1973. The Culture Bearing Unit in Cross-Cultural Surveys. *In* A Handbook of Method in Cultural Anthropology, edited by R. Naroll and R. Cohen, pp. 721-65. New York: Columbia University Press.

NELSON, C. M., 1973. Prehistoric Culture Change in the Intermontane Plateau of Western North America. *In* The Explanation of Culture Change: Models in Prehistory, edited by Colin Renfrew, pp. 371-90. Pittsburgh: University of Pittsburgh Press.

OPLER, M. E., and OPLER, C. H., 1950. Mescalero Apache History in the Southwest. New Mexico Historical Review 25:1-36.

PHELPS, A. L., 1974. An Analysis of the Ceramics of the Guadalupe Mountains National Park. Bulletin of the Texas Archeological Society 45:121-50.

RASCH, P. J. and MYERS, L., 1963. The Tragedy of the Beckwiths. The English Westerners' Brand Book, Publication No. 90, 5(4):1-6.

REEVES, C. C., Jr., 1972. Tertiary-Quaternary Stratigraphy and Geomorphology of West Texas and Southeastern New Mexico. *In* Guidebook of East-Central New Mexico, edited by V. C. Kelley and F. D. Tranger, pp. 108-17. New Mexico Geological Society, 23rd Field Conference.

RICHES, S. M., 1970. Archaeological Survey of the Eastern Guadalupe Mountains, New Mexico. Unpublished Master's thesis, Department of Anthropology, University of Wisconsin.

ROSS, J. A., 1969. Bloom Mound. Transactions of the Fifth Regional Archeological Symposium for Southeastern New Mexico and Western Texas, pp. 65-74.

RUNYAN, J., 1972. The Laguna Plata Site, LA 5148. Transactions of the Seventh Regional Archeological Symposium for Southeastern New Mexico and Western Texas, pp. 101-14.

_____, 1974. Notes on Ceramics of the Guadalupe Mountains. Unpublished manuscript.

_____, and HEDRICK, J. A., 1973. Pottery Types of the SWFAS Area. Transactions of the Eighth Regional Archeological Symposium for Southeastern New Mexico and Western Texas, pp. 19-45.

SAUER, C. O., 1971. Sixteenth Century North America. Los Angeles: University of California Press.

SCHIFFER, M. B., 1972. Archaeological Context and Systematic Context. American Antiquity 37(2):156-65.

_____, 1974. On Whallon's Use of Dimensional Analysis of Variance at Guila Naquitz. American Antiquity 39(3):490-92.

_____, and RATHJE, W. L., 1973. Efficient Exploitation of the Archeological Record: Penetrating Problems. *In* Research and Theory in Current Archeology, edited by C. L. Redman. New York: John Wiley & Sons.

SCHOENWETTER, J., 1970. Archaeological Pollen Studies on the Colorado Plateau. American Antiquity 35(1):35-48.

SCHROEDER, A., 1965. Pratt Cave Studies, Guadalupe Mountains, Texas. Unpublished manuscript on file with the National Park Service, Carlsbad National Park.

_____, 1973. The Mescalero Apaches. *In* Technical Manual: Human Systems Research. Human Systems Research.

SCHULMAN, E., 1956. Dendroclimatic Changes in Semiarid America. University of Arizona, Laboratory of Tree Ring Research.

SCHULZ, C. B., and HOWARD, E. B., 1935. The Fauna of Burnet Cave, Guadalupe Mountains, New Mexico. Proceedings of the Academy of Natural Sciences 87:273-98.

SELLARDS, E. H., 1955. Fossil Bison and Associated Artifacts from Milnesand, New Mexico. American Antiquity 20(4):336-44.

SHAFER, H. J., 1970. A Preliminary Report of an Archeological Survey in the Guadalupe Mountains National Park by the Texas Archeological Society in June, 1970. Texas Archeology 14(3):10-17.

SHUTLER, R., Jr. and SHUTLER, M. E., 1962. Archaeological Survey in Southern Nevada. Nevada State Museum Anthropological Papers No. 7.

SKINNER, S. A. and BOUSMAN, C. B., 1973. Prehistoric Archaeology in the Three-Mile and Sulfur Draw Watershed. Report submitted to the Soil Conservation Service by the Archaeology Research Program, Southern Methodist University.

_____; STEED, P.; and BEARDEN, S. E., 1974. Prehistory at Mile High. The Artifact 12(1).

SMITH, C. B.; EAST-SMITH, S.; and RUNYAN, J. W., 1966. A Preliminary Investigation of the Rattlesnake Draw Site. Lea County Archeological Society Newsletter.

SOMMER, A., 1968. Parker Ranch Ring Midden No. 1. Transactions of the Fourth Regional Archeological Symposium for Southeastern New Mexico and Western Texas, pp. 9-17.

SPAULDING, A., 1960. The Dimensions of Archaeology. *In* Essays in the Science of Culture in Honor of Leslie A. White, edited by G. E. Dole and R. L. Carneiro, pp. 437-56. Springfield: Thomas Y. Crowell.

STRUEVER, S., 1968. Problems, Methods and Organization: A Disparity in the Growth of Archaeology. *In* Anthropological Archeology in the Americas, edited by B. J. Meggers, pp. 131-51. Washington, D. C.: Anthropological Society of Washington.

THOMAS, A. B., 1959. The Mescalero Apache 1653-1874. A Report of the Mescalero-Chiricahua Land Claims Project. Contract Research No. 290-154. University of New Mexico Library.

THOMAS, D. H., 1973. An Empirical Test of Steward's Model of Great Basin Settlement Patterns. American Antiquity 38(2):155-76.

THOMAS, W. A. (editor), 1972. Indicators of Environmental Quality. New York: Olenum Press.

TRACY, F., n.d. Untitled Manuscript on file in the Maurice Garland Fulton Collections Special Collections, University of Arizona Library.

TURNER, F. J., 1920. The Frontier in American History. New York: H. Holt.

U. S. DEPARTMENT OF AGRICULTURE, 1971. Soil Survey of Eddy Area, New Mexico. U. S. Department of Agriculture, Soil Conservation Service. Washington, D. C.: U. S. Government Printing Office.

U. S. DEPARTMENT OF COMMERCE, 1971. Weather Statistics for New Mexico. Washington, D. C.: U. S. Government Printing Office.

U. S. NATIONAL RESOURCES PLANNING BOARD, 1942. The Pecos River Joint Investigation Report of Participating Agencies. Washington, D. C.: U. S. Government Printing Office.

VIVIAN, G., 1961. Gran Quivira: Excavations in a 17th Century Jumano Pueblo. National Park Service Archeological Research Series No. 8.

WARNICA, J. M. and WILLIAMSON, T., 1968. The Milnesand Site—Revisited. Transactions of the Third Regional Archeological Symposium for Southeastern New Mexico and Western Texas, pp. 21-22.

WATERFALL, U. T., 1946. Observations on the Desert Gypsum Flora of Southwestern Texas and Adjacent New Mexico. American Midland Naturalist 36:456-66.

WATT, B. K. and MERRILL, A. L., 1968. Composition of Foods. Agricultural Handbook No. 8. U. S. Department of Agriculture. Washington, D. C.: U. S. Government Printing Office.

WENDORF, F., 1961. Paleoecology of the Llano Estacado. Fort Burgwin Research Center Publication No. 1.

————, and HESTER, J. J. (editors), 1975. Late Pleistocene Environments of the Southern High Plains. Fort Burgwin Research Center Publication No. 9.

WHALLON, R. Jr., 1973. Spatial Analysis of Occupation Floors I: Application of Dimensional Analysis of Variance. American Antiquity 38(3):266-78.

————, 1974. Spatial Analysis of Occupation Floors II: The Application of Nearest Neighbor Analysis. American Antiquity 39(1):16-34.

WILLIAMS, B. J., 1974. A Model of Band Society. Memoirs of American Antiquity No. 29.

WILSON, J., 1967. Fort Sumner in 1864, Prisoners Without Walls. El Palacio 74(2):10-28.

————, 1968. Articles on Fort Sumner. De Baca County News 68(13-26).

WISEMEN, R., 1973. The Bent Highway Salvage Project, Otero County, New Mexico. Museum of New Mexico, Laboratory of Anthropology Notes 1974.

WOOD, J. E.; BICKLE, T. S.; EVANS, W.; GERMANY, J. C.; and HOWARD, V. W., 1970. The Fort Stanton Mule Deer Herd: Some Ecological and Life History Characteristics with Special Emphasis on the Use of Water. Agricultural Experiment Station Bulletin 567. Las Cruces: New Mexico State University.

ZUBROW, E., 1974. Population, Contact and Climate in the New Mexico Pueblos. University of Arizona Anthropological Paper No. 24.

SOUTHERN METHODIST UNIVERSITY
CONSTRIBUTIONS IN ANTHROPOLOGY
Available through
Archaeology Research Program
Department of Anthropology
Southern Methodist University
Dallas, Texas 75275
unless otherwise indicated

Contributions to the Prehistory of Nubia. Fred Wendorf (ed.). SMU Contributions in Anthropology No. 1. 1965. 200 pp. Price: $4.00 (Paperback)[Available through SMU Press, Dallas, Texas 75275].

Prehistory of Nubia. Fred Wendorf (ed.). SMU Contributions in Anthropology No. 2. 1968. 1,104 pp., 2 vols. (boxed), with separate Atlas. Price: $50.00 [Available through SMU Press, Dallas, Texas 75275].

Archaeological Excavations in the Fish Creek Reservoir. Dessamae Lorrain. SMU Contributions in Anthropology No. 4. 1969. Out of print.

Archaeological Investigations at the Sam Kaufman Site, Red River County, Texas. S. Alan Skinner, K. R. Harris, Keith Anderson (eds.). SMU Contributions in Anthropology No. 5. 1969. 136 pp., illus. Price: $3.50.

Archaeological Survey at Caddo Lake, Louisiana and Texas. Jon L. Gibson. SMU Contributions in Anthropology No. 6. 1970. Out of print.

Prehistoric Settlement of the DeCordova Bend Reservoir, Central Texas. S. Alan Skinner. SMU Contributions in Anthropology No. 7. 1971. Out of print.

The Archaeological Resources in the Lake Monticello Area of Titus County, Texas. Olin F. McCormick III. SMU Contributions in Anthropology No. 8. 1973. Out of print.

Botanical Survey of the Lake Monticello Area. William F. Mahler. SMU Contributions in Anthropology No. 9. 1973. 25 pp., illus. Price: $2.00.

The Historic and Prehistoric Archaeological Resources of the Squaw Creek Reservoir. S. Alan Skinner and Gerald K. Humphreys. SMU Contributions in Anthropology No. 10. 1973. 61 pp., illus. Price: $3.00.

Archaeological Investigations at Lake Palestine, Texas. Keith M. Anderson, Kathleen Gilmore, Olin F. McCormick III, and E. Pierre Morenon. SMU Contributions in Anthropology No. 11. 1974. 203 pp., illus. Price: $6.00.

Archaeological Research at Cooper Lake, 1970-1972. Robert D. Hyatt, Barbara H. Butler, and Herbert P. Mosca III. SMU Contributions in Anthropology No. 12. 1974. 93 pp., illus. Price: $5.50.

Problems in Prehistory: North Africa and the Levant. F. Wendorf and A. E. Marks (eds.). SMU Contributions in Anthropology No. 13. 1975. Price: $25.00 [Available through SMU Press, Dallas, Texas, 75275].

An Evaluation of the Archaeological Resources at Lake Whitney, Texas. S. Alan Skinner and Joseph Gallagher. SMU Contributions in Anthropology No. 14. 1974. 94 pp., illus. Price: $5.50.

Archaeological Research At Cooper Lake, Northeast Texas, 1973. Robert D. Hyatt and Karen Doehner. SMU Contributions in Anthropology No. 15. 1975. 84 pp., illus. Price: $5.50.

(Continued on next page)

Archaeological Excavations at Lake Lavon, 1974. Mark J. Lynott. SMU Contributions in Anthropology No. 16. 1975. 136 pp., illus. Price: $6.00.

Archaeological Resources at Los Esteros Lake, New Mexico. Frances Levine and Charles M. Mobley. SMU Contributions in Anthropology No. 17. 1976. 127 pp., illus. Price: $6.00.